The Port Royal Exp

The
PORT ROYAL
Experiment

A Case Study in Development

Kevin Dougherty

University Press of Mississippi / Jackson

www.upress.state.ms.us

The University Press of Mississippi is a member
of the Association of American University Presses.

Copyright © 2014 by University Press of Mississippi
All rights reserved
Manufactured in the United States of America

First printing 2014
∞
Library of Congress Cataloging-in-Publication Data

Dougherty, Kevin.
  The Port Royal Experiment : a case study in development / Kevin Dougherty.
    pages cm
    Includes bibliographical references and index.
  ISBN 978-1-62846-153-4 (cloth : alkaline paper) — ISBN 978-1-62846-154-1
(ebook) 1. African Americans—Sea Islands—History—19th century.
2. African Americans—South Carolina—Port Royal Region—History—
19th century. 3. Slaves—Emancipation—Sea Islands—History. 4. Self-
reliant living—Sea Islands—History—19th century. 5. Public-private
sector cooperation—Sea Islands—History—19th century. 6. Social
planning—Sea Islands—History—19th century. 7. Economic development—Sea Islands—History—19th century. 8. Political development—Sea
Islands—History—19th century. 9. Civil society—Sea Islands—History—
19th century. 10. Sea Islands—Social conditions—19th century. I. Title.
  E185.93.S7D68 2014
  305.896'07307579909034—dc23   2014013904

British Library Cataloging-in-Publication Data available

*This book is dedicated to all those
involved in nation building
and developmental efforts,
especially those in the military.*

Contents

The Port Royal Experiment

Introduction

The seminal work on the Port Royal Experiment remains Willie Lee Rose's 1964 *Rehearsal for Reconstruction: The Port Royal Experiment*. This present volume does not seek to compete with Rose's classic. Rather, it hopes to build on Rose's and other scholarship to present the Port Royal Experiment and the years immediately following it not as a historical narrative but as a case study of what is now called development and nation building. While the concept of development is subject to a variety of interpretations, in this context it is considered to be positive, continuously improving, and sustained change across a variety of human societal conditions. Clearly such an effort was at the heart of the Port Royal Experiment. While the term *nation building* may be slightly inappropriate given that no nation per se was the target of these efforts, the requirement to build institutions critical to nation building operations was certainly a large part of the Port Royal Experiment and offers many lessons to be learned.

The Port Royal Experiment: A Case Study in Development is divided into ten chapters, each of which is designed to treat uniquely a particular aspect of the experience. Chapter 1, "Setting the Stage for the Port Royal Experiment," provides the necessary background for the reader to understand the Port Royal Experiment and the events leading up to it. The cotton culture of the Sea Islands, the slave labor that supported it, the military operation that brought the Federal Army and Navy to the area, and the contemporary religious and philosophical institutions that influenced the developers that followed are all introduced. Chapter 2, "Planning Postcombat Operations," identifies the Federal failure to plan a sequel to the military operation and the resulting lack of preparedness to the needs of the slaves left masterless by the Confederate evacuation. In part because of this lack of a coordinated plan, a certain degree of disunity hamstrung the ad hoc effort that followed. Chapter 3, "A Survey of Philanthropic Society Activity at Port Royal," identifies the principal relief agencies, several of which were formed in specific response to the crisis, that filled the void caused by the lack of a more deliberate plan. Every organization had its own capabilities, limitations, agenda, and challenges as they struggled against difficult odds to do the best they could on behalf of the freedmen.

Chapter 4, "Development's Different Meanings to Developers and Stakeholders," explains how a fervent belief in the free labor ideology led the relief workers, who came to be known collectively as the Gideonites, to assume they understood the needs and desires of the freedmen and thus to not fully consider them as stakeholders in the development effort. A more participatory approach may have resulted in the Port Royal Experiment being more sensitive to the preferences of the freedmen and perhaps more effective. Chapter 5, "The Development of Civil Society," explores efforts to develop religion, education, self-defense, and self-government among the freedmen. Special attention is paid to the educational efforts of Laura Towne and the Penn School, generally regarded as the most successful aspect of the Port Royal Experiment. Chapter 6, "Refugees and Families," chronicles the efforts to accommodate those displaced by the war and in need of shelter on the Sea Islands. As part of this discussion, the importance of strong families within the context of development is also highlighted.

Chapter 7, "Economic Development and Land Redistribution," tackles perhaps the most difficult decision facing the Port Royal Experiment: how to develop a land policy that would reconcile the competing desires of the black and white communities. Based on this decision, the Sea Islands' blacks would either realize what they considered the most important manifestation of freedom or be returned to a status of laborer for others who owned the land. Chapter 8, "Political Development and Democratization," examines the ebb and flow of black political power not just on the Sea Islands but in all of South Carolina during Reconstruction and the early days of Redemption. In spite of the necessary expansion beyond the geographic home of the Port Royal Experiment, special attention is paid to the political career of Beaufort's Robert Smalls and the conditions that made it possible. Chapter 9, "Spoiler Problems and Resistance," explains the myriad challenges the relief agencies, the Army, the Freedmen's Bureau and other "custodians of the peace" faced from inside and outside their organizations. Ultimately, the "spoilers" did much to thwart the efforts of the Port Royal Experiment. Chapter 10, "The Hand in the Bucket: Sequencing and Perseverance," offers one explanation why the spoilers were successful. In general terms, the United States decided not to sustain its developmental effort on the Sea Islands and elsewhere in the former Confederacy. Within the Port Royal Experiment itself, the necessary institutions were not sufficiently in place before full-fledged liberalization was left to survive on its own.

Each chapter presents the case study in the context of more recent developmental and nation building efforts in places like Bosnia, Somalia, Kosovo, Iraq, and Afghanistan and incorporates recent scholarship in the field. *The Port Royal Experiment: A Case Study in Development* is designed to appeal to a wide audience with such varied interests as the Civil War, the military, nongovernmental organizations, governmental bureaucracies, African Americans, South Carolina, and nation building. In addition to these general themes, each case study is written so it can be used individually as part of an in-depth examination of a particular aspect of development. Modern readers will no doubt see that the challenges which faced the Port Royal Experiment remain relevant and their solutions remain elusive.

CHAPTER ONE

Setting the Stage for the Port Royal Experiment

The Sea Islands of South Carolina are a series of various-sized tidal and barrier islands cut by salt creeks and marshes, sounds, and rivers. Bounded by the Broad River to the west and the Coosaw River to the north, Port Royal Island lies about fifty-five miles south of Charleston, South Carolina, and about thirty-five miles north of Savannah, Georgia. At the time of the Civil War, it contained the sleepy harbor of Port Royal and the town of Beaufort, the only community of any size in the area. About two thousand people lived in Beaufort year-round, but in the summer the population would double as wealthy planters returned to occupy their stately homes. To the east of Port Royal Island, across the Beaufort River, lies Lady's Island, and southeast of that is St. Helena Island. St. Helena is about fifteen miles long and six miles wide. It is protected from Atlantic storms by a number of smaller islands, including Hunting Island. All these islands are bounded by Edisto Island, which lies across the St. Helena Sound to the north and Hilton Head Island across the Port Royal Sound to the south. Numerous other islands such as Parris, Morgan, and Eddings dot the region, and lesser waterways such as Station Creek, Trenchard's Inlet, and Morgan River wind through it.[1]

Sea Island Cotton

It was only on these Sea Islands of South Carolina and the northernmost islands of Georgia that the finer varieties of Sea Island cotton were grown. This unique product was made valuable by the length of its fibers, which when combed to their full length, measured one and a half to two inches long. Common upland or short-staple cotton could boast fibers measuring just five-eighths to one inch. Moreover, Sea Island cotton normally spun about three hundred hanks (a length of yarn 840 yards long) per pound, compared to half that number for short-staple cotton. Because of its superior strength, long-staple cotton was used for making the warp, or longitudinal threads, of many woven fabrics. As a result of these qualities, Sea Island cotton sold for at least twice as much as upland cotton. In 1860, medium-fine varieties of Sea Island cotton were selling for more than sixty cents a pound.[2] Upon learning of the economic importance of this crop, President Abraham Lincoln's attorney general, Edward Bates, wondered why the military would not launch an operation to seize the Sea Islands and their cotton, which he thought represented "merchandise ready to our hand."[3]

Such bounty did not come easily, and the care and labor involved in reaping the harvest was extensive. Expert planters selected only the finest seeds and painstakingly guarded their secrets. The preparation of the fields required heavy manuring drawn from the marsh mud. The plants needed many hoeings, performed with long, heavy cotton hoes due to the scarcity of plows. Pickers had to exercise special care to free the cotton of dirt as they picked, and the lint required special handling during its preparation for market. Bolls opened slowly, and the picking season could last six months. In the process, this long growing season subjected the crop to various natural threats such as too much or too little rain, pests, and hurricanes. The result was that raising Sea Island cotton was a year-round operation, made possible only by rigorous attention to detail and massive amounts of slave labor. In fact, by 1861, nearly 83 percent of the total Sea Islands population was made up of slaves.[4]

Unlike on the gang system of the Mississippi cotton plantations, slave labor on the Sea Islands was organized under the task system. The gang system grouped slaves of approximately equal ability together to form work parties that labored from sunrise to sundown under the supervision of a black driver. On the other hand, the task system assigned each slave a certain amount of work to be performed. On the Sea Islands, tasks came to be organized around quarter-acre sections of land laid out 105 by 105 feet.[5] If the slaves completed their tasks early, they were afforded such free time as the slave system allowed.

All manner of work could be organized using the task system. For example, "listing" was the first step in preparing the land for cotton after the field had been manured. Edward Pierce describes it as "making the bed [in which the cotton or corn is to be planted] where the alleys were at the previous raising of the crop, and the alleys being made where the beds were before." A task in this process consisted of working twenty-one or twenty-two beds in the one hundred and five foot square area. Pierce reported, "Each laborer is required to list a task and a half, or if the land is moist and heavy, a task and five or seven beds, say one-fourth or three-eighths of an acre."[6] In addition to such considerations as the condition of the soil, tasks were organized based on the kind of work involved. A task of ginning, for example, was from twenty to thirty pounds.[7]

The result was that slaves on the Sea Islands worked with less supervision than those who labored under the gang system. Also contributing to this phenomenon was the fact that most masters who could afford to do so maintained their residence at Beaufort rather than on the plantation. This arrangement left supervision of the plantation to an overseer who might also reside elsewhere. In such cases, the overseer would periodically visit to inspect work superintended by a black driver who Pierce likened "to foremen on farms in the free States."[8] While the lack of white presence no doubt brought some benefits to the slaves, Pierce felt it also meant "the negroes here have been less cared for than in most other rebel districts."[9] "Their insulation from the few currents of intelligence that find their way to the plantations of the mainland," Pierce concluded, had left the Sea Islands blacks "the lowest of their race in America."[10]

The Military Campaign

In addition to its agricultural and economic significance, from a military point of view, Port Royal Sound was the finest natural harbor on the southern seaboard. This feature made the location extremely important in light of the fact that on April 19, 1861, six days after Fort Sumter, President Lincoln had issued a proclamation declaring the blockade of the southern states from South Carolina to Texas. On April 27, the blockade was extended to Virginia and North Carolina. The purpose of the blockade was to isolate the Confederacy from European trade.

Declaring a blockade and making it effective, however, were two different things. With 189 harbor and river openings along the 3,549 miles of Confederate shoreline between the Potomac and the Rio Grande, clearly some focus was needed. This responsibility rested with the Navy Board, also called the Blockade Board, which Secretary of the Navy Gideon Welles created in June 1861 to study the conduct of the blockade and to devise ways of improving its efficiency. The Board's president was Captain Samuel Du Pont, one of the few officers in the Federal Navy who had previous experience with blockading during the Mexican War.[11] There, Du Pont had learned two key lessons: a blockading force must have enough ships to adequately cover all ports, and blockading ships had to be sustained with supplies and maintenance facilities to enable them to remain on station for extended periods. Du Pont's biographer, Kevin Weddle, notes, "These experiences would serve [Du Pont] well during the Civil War."[12]

The Board fulfilled the functions of modern day campaign plans, which are designed to arrange military operations within a given time and space to accomplish strategic and operational goals.[13] As Weddle explains, "the board created a roadmap for the Union navy to conduct a major portion of its early strategic responsibilities and stood as the role model for later naval boards and commissions."[14] Port Royal quickly drew the Board's attention.

To avoid having to lift the blockade in order to conduct resupply operations as he had experienced in Mexico, Du Pont knew he would need some strategically located land bases. At first the Federals had only Hampton Roads, Virginia, and Key West, Florida available to them. These widely separated bases made it almost impossible to maintain an effective blockade. Indeed, in the early days of the war, "some ships spent nearly as much time going to and from these bases for supply and repair as they did on blockade duty."[15] This situation would be exacerbated in foul weather, when blockading ships would need ports of refuge along the stormy Atlantic. Clearly, the Navy would need additional bases for the blockading squadron to both shut down Confederate blockade running and to resupply the Federal ships. Thus was born a strategy that would result in a series of Army-Navy operations directed against critical locations along the southern coast.

The Navy Board issued a total of seven reports, but it was its second one, presented to Welles on July 13, that concerned Port Royal. Acting on the Board's recommendations, the Federals had seized Hatteras Inlet off the coast of North Carolina in August 1861 and Ship Island, Mississippi, in September, but neither of these locations gave the fleet the large, deepwater harbor it needed in order to maintain a year-round blockade of key ports such as Wilmington, Charleston, and Savannah. Port Royal represented such a prize, both in terms of its own utility as a harbor and because from Port Royal the Federals could gain access to a series of inland waterways from which to blockade the coast from just below Charleston to the Saint Johns River in Florida without having to risk the uncertainties of the Atlantic. In effect, the Federals could block the neck of the bottle out of which the Confederate vessels had to emerge.[16]

Port Royal also supported the Navy Board's focus on the Confederate seaports that had rail or water connections with the interior.[17] Completed only in 1860, the Charleston & Savannah Railroad represented a strategic line connecting the two key cities. Although the planned Port Royal Railroad that would have intersected the Charleston & Savannah and connected Beaufort and Augusta, Georgia, was not completed until after the war, the railroad remained critical to the area. Indeed, Brigadier General Thomas Drayton, the Confederate officer in charge of the Port Royal defensive effort, was also president of the Charleston & Savannah.[18]

The Navy Board knew that Port Royal would be its biggest effort to date and that success would require a strong force. Reflecting this importance, the Board president himself, Captain Du Pont, would lead the operation. His fleet would consist of seventy-four vessels, including the Navy's best warships. Dubbed "The Great Southern Expedition" in the northern press, it represented the largest armada yet assembled under the American flag.[19]

However confident it was in its fleet, the Navy Board knew capturing a port was meaningless without an army force to then occupy the area and secure it for future operations. Still, Army of the Potomac commander Major General George McClellan objected to Du Pont's request for troops, considering the Port Royal expedition to be a sideshow and a distraction from his efforts to build his own army. President Lincoln, however, overruled McClellan and ordered that the troops be given to Du Pont. Brigadier General Thomas Sherman ("the other General Sherman") was appointed commander of this twelve-thousand-man force.[20]

On October 20, Du Pont and his fleet put out of Hampton Roads, Virginia, heading south. With northern newspapers reporting the departure, the Confederate government soon determined Du Pont's destination and alerted its coastal defenses at Port Royal. For some time, President Jefferson Davis had felt that the southern coast needed additional protection, and this new development was just the impetus he needed to act. On November 6, he reorganized the coasts of South Carolina, Georgia, and north Florida into a single department and named General Robert E. Lee as its commander.[21]

In addition to this loss of surprise, the Federals were dealt a cruel blow by the weather. On November 1, Du Pont ran into a gale off Cape Hatteras that caused two of his ships to go down and a third to have to jettison its guns to keep from sinking. By November 2, the fleet was so scattered that Du Pont could see only one other sail from the deck of his flagship, the *Wabash*. Equipment losses were heavy, including ammunition and many of the surfboats that Du Pont and Sherman had counted on to land the troops. Nonetheless, the fleet continued southward. Two days later, the weather was clear, and Du Pont dropped anchor off the bar at Port Royal. By then, twenty-five of his ships had rejoined him, and reinforcements from the squadron at Charleston and stragglers from the original party continued to filter in. Then, Du Pont spent two more days

Fort Beauregard and its eight small guns proved no match for the superior Federal firepower and maneuver at Port Royal Sound. Courtesy Library of Congress, Prints & Photographs Division, Washington, DC.

replacing the Confederate-destroyed channel markers, crossing the bar, completing his attack plan, and holding a final conference with his captains to outline his order of battle. At 8:00 a.m. on November 7, the same day Lee arrived at his new post in Charleston, Du Pont attacked.[22]

Port Royal Sound was big enough to allow maneuver, and Du Pont planned to use his steam engines to keep his ships moving in an elliptical pattern that would keep the two Confederate sand forts, Fort Walker and Fort Beauregard, under continuous fire. These positions were less than three miles apart, but their artillery was of such small caliber and inferior quality that ships could move between them and still stay out of range of both. Fort Walker was located to the south on Hilton Head and had sixteen guns mounted, most of which were thirty-two pounders. The cannon were mounted on the parapet, a measure that increased their range, but likewise increased their vulnerability. Fort Beauregard was located to the north at Bay Point and had eight small guns. Inside the forts and in the immediate vicinity were about three thousand men commanded by Brigadier General Drayton. The defenders had a blissfully uninformed confidence about them.[23]

In addition to these land defenses, Du Pont would have to contend with a small Confederate flotilla of three tugs, each mounting one gun, and a converted river steamer. Although this fleet was of dubious quality, it was commanded by Commodore Josiah Tattnall, whom Du Pont knew from "the old Navy" as a bold and capable officer. In fact, Tattnall had been Du Pont's nominal squadron commander during his voyage to China in 1857–1858 aboard the *Minnesota*. The forts, however, were Du Pont's principal concern.[24]

Originally, Du Pont had planned a joint operation to reduce the forts, but the bad weather had changed things. The three brigades under Sherman were still somewhat seasick from the rough weather, and more importantly, nearly all their landing craft had been lost in the storm. Thus, with the help of his able chief of staff, Commander Charles Davis, Du Pont developed a new plan to defeat the Confederates with the Navy alone. The Army's role would be merely to "stand by to help pick up the pieces."[25] The key to success in this Navy-only attack would be to keep the fleet moving at all times.[26]

At 8:00 a.m. on November 7, the attack began. It was a clear, calm day—ideal for delivering accurate fire from ships. Du Pont had divided his force into a main squadron of nine of his heaviest frigates and sloops and a flanking squadron of five gunboats. With the *Wabash* in the lead, the Federals entered the sound in parallel columns and began receiving fire from the forts. Du Pont's plan was for the lighter squadron to operate on the right and pass midway between the two forts, both drawing and returning fire. At a point two and a half miles beyond Fort Beauregard, the flanking squadron would turn in a circuit to the left and close in on Fort Walker, meeting it on its weakest side and simultaneously enfilading its two water faces. Once past Fort Walker, the squadrons were to swing in the direction of Fort Beauregard and repeat the elliptical pattern as often as necessary.[27] Du Pont instructed his ships to be ready to peel off and engage targets of opportunity, to include the Confederate ships, as they presented themselves.

As this maneuver was unfolding, Tattnall brought his Confederate flotilla down the sound and engaged the *Wabash*. Du Pont's right column was positioned for just such a contingency, and as the six gunboats gave chase, Tattnall beat a hasty retreat three miles northwest of Fort Walker and took refuge at the mouth of Skull Creek. Dipping his pennant three times as a salute to his old messmate, Tattnall was bottled up by the Federal gunboats and out of the fight for good.[28]

In the meantime, the main Federal squadron was executing its elliptical pattern, advancing about two miles beyond the entrance of the sound on the Fort Beauregard side and then turning left and returning on the Fort Walker side. Such a course gave the ships the advantage of opening fire on the inland and weaker side of the fort and of enfilading the main battery before coming abreast of it. With each pass, the squadron widened its course so as to bring its guns closer to the target. These constant changes in speed, range, and deflection made the Federal fleet extremely hard for the Confederate gunners to engage.[29] One Confederate lamented, "No sooner did we obtain [the enemy's] range when it would be changed, and time after time rechanged, while the deep water permitted him to choose his position and fire shot after shot and shell after shell, with the precision of target practice."[30] With a bit of understatement, E. A. Pollard admits that "this manoeuvre doubtless disturbed the aim of the artillerists in the forts."[31]

To make matters worse, the Confederate gunners had more problems than just the moving targets. They were low on ammunition, and some of what they had was the wrong size for their guns. Additionally, they had inferior powder and defective fuses.[32] Drayton confessed to being unable to provide "not a ripple upon the broad expanse of water to disturb the accuracy of fire from the broad decks of that magnificent armada ... advancing in battle array to vomit forth its iron hail with all the spiteful energy of long-suppressed rage and conscious strength."[33] The Confederates were clearly at a disadvantage.

But what had made this so, even more than the disparity in arms, was Du Pont's brilliant scheme of maneuver. Fort Walker had been built to defend against an attacking force moving straight in from the sea. Thus, its northern flank was its weakest, a fact that Du Pont had learned from reconnaissance. Du Pont's plan took full advantage of this condition.

The Federal firepower was staggering. The *Wabash* alone fired 880 rounds and the *Susquehanna* added 750 more. At one point as many as sixty heavy shells a minute, ranging in size from eight to eleven inches, descended on Fort Walker.[34] Confederate resistance did not last long against such an onslaught. As Du Pont began his third ellipse, he received word that Fort Walker had been abandoned. At 2:20 p.m., a naval landing party raised the United States flag over the wreckage, and by nightfall Army troops had landed and occupied the fort. Fort Beauregard, which was merely an adjunct to Fort Walker, ceased firing at 3:35 p.m. and lowered its flag at sunset. Knowing Fort Walker had fallen and fearful of being cut off, the defenders of Fort Beauregard withdrew to safety. Early the next morning, Federal troops crossed the water and occupied the position. In the words of Shelby Foote, for the Confederates "the fight had been lost from the moment Du Pont had conceived his plan of attack."[35]

The Federals lost eight killed and twenty-three wounded. The Confederates lost about one hundred total. The victory gave the Federals an excellent harbor that became the home base for the South Atlantic Blockading Squadron for the remainder of the war. Moreover, it struck a blow in both the sentimental heartland of secession and in an important cotton-producing region. Within three days, the Federals moved up the rivers and inlets and occupied the towns of Beaufort and Port Royal. The Federals were now in a position to threaten either Charleston or Savannah, and the local population was thrown into a panic. Nearly the entire white population fled, leaving large numbers of their slaves behind. By December, planters along the Georgia–South Carolina coast were burning cotton to prevent its capture.[36]

The new department commander, General Robert E. Lee, had arrived too late to do anything about Port Royal, but he accepted its lessons and made adjustments as he could. Concluding that a Federal attack "can be thrown with great celerity against any point, and far outnumbers any force we can bring against it in the field," Lee knew the Confederacy simply was not strong enough to defend the entire coast.[37] Instead, he initiated three measures designed to focus the limited Confederate resources where they would do the most good. These were to strengthen the defenses at Fort Pulaski, Georgia, and Charleston in order to withstand a more serious bombardment, to obstruct the waterways that might be used by Federal ships, and to assemble the scattered Confederate forces at the most probable points of Federal attack.[38] Later, Lee would put into effect a longer-range plan by ordering the withdrawal inland of garrisons and guns on outlying positions. This move was part of Lee's plan to hold only key locations such as Charleston. Finally, at Savannah and along the southern part of the Charleston & Savannah Railroad, Lee built a strong defensive line upon which he could concentrate his forces. This tactic would force the Federal Army to fight without the assistance of its powerful Navy while at the same time allowing the Confederates to move troops and supplies by rail from Charleston or Savannah to be concentrated at the threatened point.[39] Finally, at Savannah and along the southern part of the Charleston & Savannah Railroad, Lee built a strong defensive line upon which he could concentrate his forces. This tactic would force the Federal Army to fight without the assistance of its powerful Navy[40] In spite of these efforts, the advantage clearly lay with the Federals.

As Lee readjusted his defensive plan, Sherman briefly considered sending his troops inland and turning "left or right to one of the cities."[41] Doing so would have presented the Confederates with the prospect of a three-front war, but in spite of his reputation for driving his men hard, Sherman was deterred by "the winding and shallow creeks" and the inexperience of his troops. He did not press his advantage and therefore missed an opportunity. In fact, from the Army point of view, the battle of Port Royal Sound was largely inconsequential in that the Federals never used the port to stage a major offensive. Bern Anderson writes that "the war might have taken an entirely different course if the Army had chosen to exploit its opportunities in that region."[42] Instead, Theodore Rosengarten concludes that "what was lost, therefore, in November, 1861, was not the strategic position both sides imagined it to be, but simply the homeland of the old Sea Island families."[43]

This demographic change, however, was in itself very important. The flight of the Confederate population left in its wake some ten thousand now masterless slaves unprepared for this welcome but unexpected development. If the Federal military did not fully exploit the Port Royal victory, hosts of social activists did. With the sudden departure of their masters, many blacks were faced with a future for which they had no way of being prepared. Soon many Northerners with a strong moral commitment to abolition descended on the Sea Islands to help the former slaves transition to freedom.

Abolitionist Sentiment and Organization

A wave of religious revivals swept the northern United States in the late 1820s, and in addition to elevating spiritual awareness, they also inspired a new sense of urgency in the abolitionist movement. Bostonian William Lloyd Garrison became the champion of the doctrine of "immediacy," which embraced an immediate moral commitment to emancipation. Increasingly, abolitionists called upon all Americans to recognize a Christian duty to view slavery as a deprivation of a human being's God-given right to be free moral beings.[44] Denominations all across the religious spectrum embraced this call, including the humanist Unitarians and the more traditional Methodists. This mix of abolition and religion would be well represented during the Port Royal Experiment.

One of the results of Garrison's efforts to coalesce the antislavery elements in the East was the founding of the New England

Anti-Slavery Society in 1832. Building on this momentum, Garrison made a resolution in Boston on January 21, 1833, to form a national society. The result was the American Anti- Slavery Society, which was founded at a convention held in Philadelphia on December 4, 1833. With this development, Maine, New Hampshire, and Vermont withdrew from the New England Society and formed their own local state organizations. What was left of the New England Society decided to limit its operations to Massachusetts, and by 1834 it became the Massachusetts Anti-Slavery Society.

The strong influence of Garrison on this new organization is reflected in the demand of the Constitution of the Massachusetts Anti-Slavery Society for the immediate abolition of slavery. This interpretation meant not only freedom but the eradication of all vestiges of slavery, including all discriminatory laws, social customs, and practices. The goal of the Massachusetts Anti-Slavery Society was to obtain for blacks equal civil and political rights and privileges.[45] This organization represented a ready resource to rally to the needs and opportunities that presented themselves after the Federal victory at Port Royal. Another connection between the Massachusetts Anti-Slavery Society and Port Royal was that Edward Philbrick, who became the Sea Islands' most prominent superintendent, was the son of Samuel Philbrick, who had served as the organization's treasurer.[46]

Religiously, Philbrick aligned himself with the Unitarians, a group of largely well-educated and affluent New Englanders who believed in the essential goodness of humanity. For the Unitarians, Jesus was a mortal man rather than the Son of God and, as their name would indicate, they rejected the concept of the Trinity. God was seen as a merciful, loving father, and mankind was capable of goodness and virtue through the development of a Christian character. Rejecting not only orthodox Calvinism, the Unitarians were skeptical of any elaborate theological system, instead urging each individual to search the Scriptures and find the truth. Once discovered, Unitarians emphasized that this individual enlightenment must not be turned into dogma to be imposed on others, and they encouraged toleration of differences among devout men and women.[47] Among the key Unitarians associated with the Port Royal Experiment were William Gannett and Laura Towne.

While Unitarianism enjoyed a small but devoted following, most Protestants embraced a softened version of orthodox Calvinism such as that represented by Methodism. Inspired by the preaching of John Wesley, Methodism represented a very practical and socially active theology that emphasized scriptural passages that demonstrated the manifestation of Christian faith by works.[48] An example would be Matthew 25: 35–36, which notes, "For I was an hungred, and ye gave me meat: I was thirsty, and ye gave me drink: I was a stranger, and ye took me in. Naked, and ye clothed me: I was sick, and ye visited me: I was in prison, and ye came unto me."[49] Wesley argued that such "works of mercy" constitute "real means of grace" and are "necessary to salvation."[50] This concern for the human condition led Wesley to argue in his 1774 *Thoughts Upon Slavery* that the very law of nature affirms liberty as the right of every individual. He rhetorically asked the slave trader, "What is your heart made of? Is there no such principle as Compassion there? Do you never *feel* another's pain? Have you no Sympathy? No sense of human woe? No pity for the miserable?"[51] (emphasis in original). This mix of abolitionist sentiment and social activism attracted many Methodists such as Mansfield French to the Sea Islands.

It was the mix of these agricultural, economic, military, societal, and religious factors that combined to launch what became known as the Port Royal Experiment. Under its auspices, the region became the cradle of South Carolina's first black schools and free labor initiatives and a fertile recruiting ground for black soldiers. Although the Emancipation Proclamation was yet to come, the Port Royal Experiment helped place the war in a broader moral consciousness. W. Scott Poole writes, "Secession may have begun on the South Carolina coast but it is as true that in this same region the war for the Union became the war against slavery."[52] With this new front came a bold social experiment that, if successful, its primary architect envisioned "may anywhere else be hopefully attempted."[53]

CHAPTER TWO

Planning Postcombat Operations

The developmental effort that followed the Federal victory at Port Royal was plagued by planning deficiencies that led to confusion and disjointed effort among its participants. Willie Lee Rose contends whatever the developers' good intentions, their efforts "misfired, as often as not through lack of a coordinated plan conceived early enough to become an effective pattern of postwar reconstruction."[1] Similar failures to plan subsequent phases to military operations, act quickly, and ensure unity of effort among participants continued to plague recent U.S. efforts in Iraq, Kosovo, and Somalia, and the Port Royal Experiment serves as a cautionary tale for those planning such transitions from combat operations to nation building activities.

Branches and Sequels

Kevin Weddle notes that the Navy Board was a "largely successful attempt by the United States Navy to produce a military (naval) strategy that was fully coordinated with the national strategy and government policies."[2] Yet in spite of its significant successes, to include this one at Port Royal, the Board has been criticized for not developing concrete ideas for how to exploit the capture of Confederate ports in subsequent operations.[3] Today's military planners address this requirement by arranging operations to include branches and sequels. Branches are options built into the basic plan. They add flexibility to plans by anticipating situations that could alter the basic plan as a result of enemy action, availability of friendly capabilities or resources, or even a change in weather. Related to the branch is the sequel. A sequel is a subsequent operation based on possible outcomes—victory, defeat, or stalemate—of the current operation.[4] While the Navy Board planned other aspects of the blockade very well, a consistent shortcoming was the absence of any semblance of branches and sequels in its efforts. There certainly was no sequel planned for the phase to follow the successful seizure of Port Royal. While the Navy Board must take responsibility for having failed to plan a military exploitation, the sudden success caught other elements of the Lincoln administration struggling for a response to the situation as well.

The Contraband Policy

For the Sea Island blacks, the flight of their masters ushered in a period of what was called "confusion" as they tried to make sense of their new situation.[5] The Federal authorities also were unprepared to deal with this development. A major part of the problem was President Abraham Lincoln's reluctance to address decisively the matter of slavery, he having initially declared that the war was based solely on the objective of preserving the Union. The issue had been forced in August 1861 when Major General John Fremont proclaimed emancipation in areas under his military control in Missouri. The politically aware Lincoln, cognizant of the fact that he could ill afford to alienate the four slaveholding states that remained loyal to the Union, reversed the initiative. Still, the fact that slavery contributed to the Confederate war effort was a very practical concern that demanded attention from a military if not moral point of view.

A practical alternative was presented by Major General Benjamin Butler when runaway slaves began entering his lines at Fort Monroe, Virginia. Knowing the slaves had been used to build Confederate fortifications, Butler used existing international law to declare them "contraband of war" and refused to return them to the Confederates. Although an incomplete and problematic solution, Butler's tactic was extremely useful in justifying the retention of refugee slaves without unduly agitating political sentiments in the Union's slaveholding border states. War Department communications soon began using the convenient term, and the newly masterless Sea Island blacks fell under this practice of being now neither slave nor free, but contraband property subject to seizure by Federal authorities.[6] As abandoned Confederate property, the contrabands became the responsibility of Secretary of the Treasury Salmon Chase who, without benefit of much guidance or authority from the president or Congress, wrestled with deciding upon a proper course to follow.[7]

"The Golden Hour"

This underdeveloped policy stands in sharp contrast with nation building expert James Dobbins's contention that "perhaps most importantly, the intervening authorities need to arrive with a carefully thought out set of mission objectives commensurate with the resources to be committed and appropriate for the challenges to be confronted."[8] He acknowledges that no plan can reliably plot an operation from start to finish and that unexpected challenges doubtlessly arise. The effective plan, however, "assembles the necessary resources and establishes objectives achievable within those limits" while providing the "flexibility to meet …challenges as they develop."[9] No such plan existed to guide the Port Royal Experiment.

Dobbins notes the existence of a "golden hour" in the weeks immediately following the arrival of intervening forces in which the situation is "highly malleable." In order to properly shape this opportunity, the intervening force will need at its immediate disposal a minimum set of assets to include security forces, civil administrators, humanitarian workers, and funding.[10] Instead, the Port Royal Experiment was comprised of belatedly assembled and uncertain resources that arrived after Dobbins's golden hour had passed. For example, Laura Towne, one of the early relief workers on the scene, was pleased when the eventual arrival of rations of pork caused "great joy," but she also noted, "If this had only come when first ordered there would have been this

goodwill and trust from the first." While appreciative of the shipment of supplies, she could not help but lament the "immense
good" it could have done "if it had come in season."[11]

An example of a task Dobbins requires be addressed early is
the "reintegration of former combatants."[12] The departure of the
Confederate population from the Port Royal area made this process unnecessary, but it was replaced by the need to transition the
former slaves into the economy as free laborers. With no working
system in place to guide action, one superintendent charged with
organizing plantation labor complained, "general plans are usu-
ally determined just too late."[13] The lesson is that timing is critical
and planning helps make that possible.

Three Competing Proposals

In the absence of a planned sequel to the Port Royal military
campaign, "a hundred theorists came forward with plans, solutions, and panaceas to be tried out."[14] What planning did precede
the Port Royal Experiment was largely the result of disjointed,
individual, and often competing effort. Frederick Law Olmsted,
William Reynolds, and Edward Pierce all developed plans, each
of which had its own political sponsors. Each plan also represented its own view of how the situation on the Sea Islands
should develop. Rose concludes, "The essential problem was
that the disputing parties had differing perspectives on the New
Canaan. Each saw a vision, and each party regarded the other as
impractical-and visionary."[15] The resulting competition created a
lack of unity of effort among the participants.

Olmsted was the most anticipatory of the three would-be
architects of what would become the Port Royal Experiment. His
interest in the task of transitioning the black population from
slaves to citizens dated to his first trip to the South as a reporter
for the *New York Times* in 1852. Olmsted saw the problem as
being how to reverse the dehumanizing aspects of slavery. By
1856, he had published a plan that called for gradual and com-
pensated emancipation by which slaves could earn and purchase
their freedom while simultaneously learning how to live with it.[16]

Shortly after the outbreak of the Civil War, Olmsted had unsuccessfully requested government employment as commissioner of contrabands. In August, he made a proposal for management of the contrabands to Major General George McClellan, but this effort also came for naught.[17] In spite of the attempts of Olmsted and others, there was no official policy in place to handle the situation that was now unfolding at Port Royal.

Given the lack of guidance from President Lincoln, Secretary Chase tackled the easier problem of contraband cotton before trying to figure out what to do with the contraband slaves. In December, he was approached by Lieutenant Colonel William Reynolds wore bore the recommendation of Chase's friend, the Rhode Island governor William Sprague. In addition to being an officer in the First Rhode Island Artillery, Reynolds had "for many years occupied the most prominent position in the cotton trade." Sprague, too, was a cotton manufacturer, and Chase trusted his judgment. By December 20, Reynolds was in Beaufort as the United States agent to collect cotton.[18]

In the meantime, Olmsted was laboring as executive secretary of the United States Sanitary Commission at the time Du Pont seized Port Royal, and Olmsted learned from a Sanitary Commission agent that no sufficient government plan was directing the effort there. After calling upon Secretary of War Edwin Stanton and Secretary of the Treasury Chase without satisfaction, Olmsted turned to Senator Lafayette Foster of Connecticut, who expressed interest in Olmsted's ideas. Foster asked Olmsted to prepare a bill outlining a plan that Foster could then introduce to the Senate.[19]

The bill Olmsted came up with included short- and long-term policies. The immediate concern was to protect the blacks from hunger and disease. Beyond that, the bill provided for training in the fundamental duties as free men, self-support without dependence on charity, family obligations, and the rightful authority of law.[20] Of critical note was the provision that all activities would be conducted under the jurisdiction of the War Department.[21]

Olmsted's bill would be implemented by a three-man board of commissioners appointed by the president to manage all lands committed to them by military authorities. The commissioners had a twofold role. With regard to the plantations, they would act as receivers in bankruptcy. With regard to the contrabands, they would serve like guardians to the poor. All money derived from the sale of cotton would go toward operating the plantations rather than charity, education, or moral training of the blacks. The commissioners were, however, empowered to help the contrabands help themselves and to facilitate the work of benevolent societies.[22]

Recognizing the fleeting nature of the "golden hour," Olmsted avoided any mention of controversial matters that might prolong debate, such as the legal status of the contrabands. This tactic had the advantage of getting the plan in motion to facilitate the needs of the agricultural cycle as well as allowing the government to determine a considered policy "in its own good time." Foster was impressed by Olmsted's work, and he introduced it to the Senate on February 14.[23]

By this time Secretary Chase, with Reynolds taking care of the cotton problem, had turned his attention to the humanitarian one and called Boston attorney Edward Pierce to Washington to receive instructions for a mission to Port Royal. A friend of Senator Charles Sumner, Pierce had become Chase's private secretary after graduating from Harvard Law School in 1852. He had also been a delegate to the Republican Convention that nominated Abraham Lincoln in 1860.

When the Civil War broke out, Pierce enlisted as a private in the Third Massachusetts Regiment, and during this time he supervised contrabands who had entered Federal lines at Fort Monroe. He recorded these experiences in an article called "The Contrabands at Fort Monroe" that was published in the November 1861 issue of the *Atlantic Monthly* and expressed Pierce's favorable assessment of the blacks' capabilities, industry, and suitability for military service.[24]

Chase picked Pierce for the Port Royal assignment because he knew Pierce would be sensitive to the welfare of the contrabands but also because he considered Pierce to be a man of "cool and sound" judgment who would render a thoughtful evaluation, rather than one based on "mere sympathy." The end result of Pierce's efforts, Chase advised, would be to prepare the Sea Islands blacks "for self-support by their own industry hereafter."[25]

Pierce left New York for Port Royal on January 13. Almost as soon as he arrived, he began to take issue with Reynolds's plan to employ several cotton collectors who would be paid a commission based on the amount of product they each secured. The cotton would then be shipped to New York for ginning. Pierce objected to this procedure that would increase employment in the North but leave the Sea Island blacks wanting. It quickly became apparent to Pierce that the rapid collection and shipment of cotton was Reynolds's "controlling consideration," while Pierce thought the black population should be the principal concern.[26] Instead, he found some of the cotton agents practicing what he considered to be a "reign of terror over the Negroes."[27]

Pierce understood the urgency of the situation. If the labor situation was not resolved soon, there would be no cotton crop in 1862. Equally important, as long as the blacks were idle, they would have to be supported by charity, a condition that did not further the cause of emancipation or meet Chase's charge to prepare the blacks "for self-support by their own industry."[28] On February 3, Pierce submitted his report to Chase; it called for superintendents to be appointed for the plantations that would use "paternal discipline" to direct the work of the black population.[29] He also noted, "As part of the plan proposed, missionaries will be needed to address the religious element of a race so emotional in their nature, exhorting to all practical virtues, and inspiring the laborers with a religious zeal for faithful labor, the good nurture of their children, and for clean and healthful habits." Pierce counted on "the benevolence of the Free States" to provide these missionaries, but he also felt "the Government should, however, provide some teachers specially devoted to teaching reading, writing and arithmetic, say some twenty-five, for the territory now occupied by our forces, and private benevolence might even be relied on for these."[30] Having been in Port Royal just a few weeks, in mid-February, Pierce returned north to champion his plan, well aware of Reynolds's alternative proposal.[31]

Reynolds's plan had the advantage of simplifying the matter for the government by leasing the plantations and laborers to a

private organization. Additionally, it held the promise of immediate revenue, something the cash-strapped government could
sorely use. Reynolds had included certain humanitarian considerations for the laborers such as free housing, clothes, and food;
a chance to attend school during three months of the year; and
a low wage. However, Pierce knew these token inducements did
not add up to a free status. He also recognized the dangers of personal temptation inherent in Reynolds's plan. "No man, not even
the best of men," Pierce argued, "charged with the duties which
ought to belong to the guardians of these people, should be put
in a position where there would be such a conflict between his
humanity and self-interest." Taking the long view, Pierce considered the immediate revenue promised by Reynolds's plan to be
of little consequence compared to the opportunity to launch "a
beneficent system which will settle a great social question, insure
the sympathies of foreign nations, now wielded against us, and
advance the civilization of the age."[32]

Pierce's arguments resonated with Chase, who endorsed
Pierce's plan and sent him to see President Lincoln on February
15. The president seemed irritable and distracted during Pierce's
visit and wondered why Pierce was "itching" to get the blacks
inside Federal lines. When Pierce explained that the contrabands
had always lived where they currently were and it was their masters who had run away, Lincoln wrote a short note to Chase, tell-
ing him to give Pierce "in his discretion . . . such instructions in
regard to Port Royal as may seem judicious."[33]

With that scant endorsement, Pierce tried to enlist congressional support for his plan but found little interest. Aside from
Chase, the only other person Pierce talked to in Washington that
appreciated the need for a policy was Olmsted, who continued
to pursue a plan that would be based on authority established
by Congress rather than merely assumed by the secretary of the
Treasury.[34] In spite of Foster's backing, Olmsted found no more
enthusiasm in Congress than did Pierce. While the Foster bill
languished, Chase satisfied himself with Pierce's plan, and on
February 19 he appointed Pierce superintendent of all employees on the Sea Islands plantations. Less than two weeks later,
Pierce sailed for Port Royal, carrying with him a weakly worded

letter from Secretary of War Stanton recommending Pierce to the military authorities and asking them to give him whatever assistance as was convenient, given their wartime operational requirements. Accompanying Pierce was the first contingent of the missionaries and teachers that would come to be known as the Gideonites. This group had been raised by various relief organizations which would continue to pay them until the government could assume part of the expense from proceeds gained by sale of the cotton crop.

Rose credits the Gideonites with filling a void left by "such inadequate and tardy plans as the Administration adopted."[35] Laura Roper notes that the Port Royal Experiment began "under divided and dubious authority and supported by private philanthropy."[36] Even Pierce admits, "In every sense it was an experiment,— the object indefinite, the method and means untried; it was simply a generous and ready response to a cry for help."[37] Much of these inauspicious circumstances were the result of the failure to plan a sequel to Du Pont's Port Royal Campaign that would facilitate the transition to postcombat operations.

In spite of Pierce's departure for Port Royal, Olmsted continued his efforts to garner a clear policy. Even Pierce admitted he had more responsibility than he had plan, complaining he was "troubled with men who proposed a grand system for me. I tell them I have none, that I don't look ahead the length of my nose— and am content with doing each day's work."[38] When Laura Towne expressed her desire not "to interfere with the system," Pierce replied, "Oh, Miss Towne, we have no systems here."[39]

Some relief seemed in the offing when the Foster bill finally passed the Senate on March 3, and Olmsted further advanced his plan in a letter to President Lincoln on March 8. But while Olmsted was organizing support for the bill in the House, Secretary Chase sent for him and expressed his lack of interest in the bill. Instead, Chase asked Olmsted to consider assuming Pierce's duties at Port Royal. Pierce had all along hoped to be relieved in April, and on March 29 he wrote Olmsted a letter noting he expected to welcome Olmsted any day as his successor. In the meantime, the Boston Educational Committee, the National Freedmen's Relief Association, and the Port Royal

Relief Association had offered Olmsted the position as general agent of their philanthropies in Port Royal.[40]

Out of deference to Chase, Olmsted had asked his congressional supporters to be inactive on Foster's bill while Olmsted weighed these developments. However, just when it seemed all was in order for Olmsted to report to Port Royal, the entire plan fell apart. What exactly happened remains a mystery, but it appears Olmsted came to believe that the authority necessary to do what he envisioned could come only from the military authority of Secretary of War Stanton and not from Chase. Olmsted took the matter to Stanton who appeared poised to appoint Olmsted military governor of the Sea Islands when Chase intervened. Chase argued he had already bestowed such a position on Pierce.[41]

Olmsted was philosophical about his change in fortune, stating, "I believe it paid, though the study and energy I gave to the matter did not accomplish the precise result, or anything like as good a result, as I meant it should."[42] Thus, the Foster bill fell by the wayside, leaving Laura Roper to lament, "what might have happened had Olmsted's policy been adopted is one of history's undisclosed alternatives."[43]

Lack of Unity

One of the strengths Roper considers to have been inherent in the Olmsted plan was that the War Department would have had sole jurisdiction for operations at Port Royal.[44] Instead, she contends the Port Royal Experiment was "conducted under the divided and often conflicting authority of the War and Treasury departments and hampered by frictions among various agents at the scene."[45] A lack of unity of effort plagued the operation, and at least part of the U.S. government's ineffective planning effort can be explained by Pierce's argument that it was impossible "for one not personally versed with affairs at Port Royal, to find out what should be done, as the officials and others there disagree so much among themselves."[46] Indeed, it appeared that "there were too many chiefs and too few Indians at Port Royal," where "everybody wanted the leading part in conducting the freedmen to the promised land."[47] The result, as described by C. Vann Woodward, was that "organized groups struggled against each other for the allegiance of the slaves, the support of the military, and the backing of Washington authorities."[48] Thus, one Gideonite who expected to "find peace and zeal down here—a band of fellow workers living in harmony and working with combined effort," instead found "friction in every quarter—military, religious, and political."[49] Among the key conflicts were those between the Gideonites and the cotton speculators, among the Gideonites themselves, and between the military and the Gideonites.

Tension between the Gideonites and the cotton agents arose early. Pierce's orders from Secretary Chase instructed him to report to Colonel Reynolds, who was already at Port Royal. Pierce had been a private in the army, and he understood how a subordinate relationship with Reynolds would hamstring Pierce's efforts. Instead of showing Reynolds his letter from Chase, Pierce quickly requested new orders from Chase that would put him on an equal level with Reynolds. Pierce explained to Chase that he needed a completely free hand in conducting his investigations.[50]

As Pierce suspected, he soon found himself in conflict with Reynolds. Even with Pierce's nominal backing by the Treasury Department and the at least grudging cooperation of the Army, Reynolds still had the benefit of preceding Pierce in the area. Empowered to confiscate not just cotton, but furniture, livestock, and everything "movable," Reynolds's agents had deprived Pierce of the basic essentials he needed to establish his operation. Towne reported "many" cotton agents were "using Government horses and carriages, furniture, corn, garden vegetables, etc." She declared the practice "too bad."[51] Pierce protested vigorously to Reynolds, and a standoff ensued. At the heart of the matter was the fact that in order to do his job, Pierce needed the furniture, livestock, and farm equipment Reynolds controlled, and in order to do his job, Reynolds needed the labor which Pierce controlled.[52]

William Gannett was among the original group of Gideonites that set sail for Port Royal on March 3, 1862, and he quickly noted the cool reception his group received from the cotton agents. Meeting "open & secret opposition from these cotton-agents,"

Gannett was not surprised because the "whole business of our commission & all its agents are much disliked by the cotton agents,— partly because they don't sympathize with our purposes, partly because we seem about to usurp their authority,— to which of course we do succeed." Gannett felt there was little hope for "any regularity & real improvement till we are delivered from our cotton agent, and the influences which emanate from him and his interests."[53]

Indeed, the conflict only worsened, with Towne representing the Gideonite contention that "the cotton agents have been a great trouble and promise still to be."[54] She accused them of "evil doings generally," and specifically objected to their overcharging the blacks for goods and "imposing upon the negroes shamefully." In return, she reported the agents "hate this whole Society of Superintendents, etc., who will not see the negroes wronged."[55] Clearly, relations between the Gideonites and the cotton agents had devolved into perpetual bickering.

The complaints of Pierce and others eventually reached Chase, who ordered Reynolds to meet with Pierce. One of the most abusive agents was Colonel William Nobles, who was so angered by the charges that he physically assaulted Pierce on May 7.[56] Military authorities intervened and sent Nobles north "in disgrace," while Pierce protested to Chase, who had not become involved in hopes that Reynolds would soon finish collecting the cotton and that his job and presence in Port Royal would be ended. Even after this eventuality came to pass, Chase still found himself dealing with the results of Reynolds's unscrupulous and fraudulent dealings.[57] At least for Pierce, the conflict was over, but the U.S. government continued to pay a price for the lack of planning that had allowed Reynolds to fill the vacuum at Port Royal.

Even with Reynolds's departure, the Gideonites still experienced a degree of cross-purposes among themselves. The eclectic nature of the group not surprisingly resulted in members with different ideas, philosophies, approaches, and visions. Even among the missionaries, there was a degree of tension and competition that Rose describes as "a straw in a wind that . . . nearly reached the dimensions of a gale."[58] Much of these differences were based on the geographical origin of the group.

Sent at the request of the American Missionary Association, Reverend Mansfield French had arrived on the Sea Islands about a week before Pierce, and the two men quickly found common cause in their suspicions of the cotton agents and in their belief that the contrabands could rise to the demands of freedom. The pair agreed on a division of labor by which French would focus on New York City and Pierce on Boston in rallying support for the plan Pierce was preparing for Secretary Chase.[59] Abolitionist sentiment had developed along two different paths in these two locations. In Boston and elsewhere in New England, anti-slavery thought was firmly grounded in ethical principles, but it had grown outside the organization of the church. In New York, on the other hand, evangelicalism had been a primary force in the abolitionist movement. The result was that by the time representatives from the two groups reached Port Royal, they "were markedly different in temperament and in the special sources of their inspiration."[60]

Their evangelical background gave the New Yorkers a distinct advantage with the Sea Islanders, whose Closed-Communion Baptist heritage emphasized emotional revivals and conversions and who greatly preferred preaching about the saving power of Jesus to moral lectures on truth, duty, cleanliness, and the like.[61] The Bostonians, especially the well represented Unitarians among them, considered such outward displays as excessive and unproductive. They often considered the blacks' religious practice to take up too much of their time and to be unnecessary distractions from cooking, learning, or fieldwork. French understood the phenomenon and reported to Secretary Chase "the Unitarians don't get hold of things in the right way, for the people are mostly Baptist, and like emotional religion better than rational, so called."[62] French's critics, however, considered him "too Methodistical in matter and manner, appealing too much to the Religious sentiment of the people and not aiming sufficiently to strengthen them in principle and purpose."[63] The result was the two groups sometimes "quarreled ignominiously among themselves as they took sides in the freedmen's church disputes, each attempting to spread his own sect or to enlarge his following."[64] One such example occurred when a freedmen Baptist congregation on St. Helena Island decided, with some coaching from their northern Baptist minister, to institute "closed communion," thereby excluding the Unitarian teachers and superintendents on the island from the proceedings.[65] The rivalry was such that Towne reported the "intense horror" of one minister when he learned she was a Unitarian.[66]

Accusations flew between the Boston and New York contingents concerning each other's qualifications and motives, and some missionaries chose not to associate with members of the other group.[67] The New Englanders, with some justification, claimed their teachers were better qualified and assumed a superior attitude.[68] Indications of misconduct fueled this perception. Unfortunately, some dubious missionaries were sent to Port Royal, and when these "rotten apples" were caught in some indiscretion, the Bostonians indiscriminately consigned the offender to "one of the French set."[69]

A third group was added to the mix when the Port Royal Relief Committee was organized in Philadelphia. The initial ship from this group set sail in April 1862 with a cargo of clothing. Soon the organization broadened its purpose beyond distribution of immediate humanitarian aid to attempting to teach the Sea Islanders "the rudimentary arts of civilized life" and "to instruct them in the elements of an English education and the simple truths of the Bible divested as much as possible of all sectarian bias."[70] The Pennsylvanians often took a middle ground between the Bostonians and New Yorkers.[71]

Among the causes of friction plaguing the three groups was their competition for support. The New England and Pennsylvania societies established branch units in various towns. Each branch supported a teacher by paying her salary and corresponding with her. This method stimulated local interest and reduced administrative costs. The New Yorkers, on the other hand, dispatched paid lecturers, often into New England and Pennsylvania, where the societies there viewed them as unwelcome competition in raising funds. Additionally, all three societies battled each other for overseas contributions from England.[72]

Such rivalries frustrated early attempts at cooperation among the three societies, although initial enthusiasm helped "enforce a grudging cooperation if it could not stop the quarreling."[73] It was not until May 1865 that they joined forces by forming the Freedmen's Aid Society, united in large measure by the cause of black suffrage.[74]

While this unification helped improve cooperation among the Gideonites, tension between the Gideonites and the military remained an issue. Rose believes that "most army officers were resentful of the Port Royal mission, looking upon Pierce's band as interlopers who had come before the situation was ripe for them."[75] One in particular marveled at what he considered the Gideonites' "crude and extravagant notions" that he expressed pride in "modifying."[76] Soldiers derided the missionaries as "nigger-lovers" who would "run away at the first danger."[77] Thus, Towne believed the Gideonites were compelled to keep their antislavery views "in the background for fear of exciting the animosity of the army, and we are only here by the military's sufferance."[78] Indeed, the Gideonites found that "the army officers in sympathy with their undertaking, at its outset, were very few."[79]

Even Brigadier General Rufus Saxton, who many Gideonites considered a "thoroughgoing Abolitionist of the radical sort," was not immune from the tensions between the missionaries and the military. Secretary of War Stanton had ordered Saxton to Port Royal on April 29, 1862 to "take possession of all the plantations heretofore occupied by the rebels, and take charge of all the inhabitants remaining thereon within the department, or which the fortunes of war may hereafter bring into it," with full authority to make "such rules and regulations for the cultivation of the land, and for the protection, employment and government of the inhabitants as circumstances seem to require."[80] Ostensibly powerful, Saxton would report only to the War Department and to Department of the South commander Major General David Hunter. Raised in "the free air of the valley of the Connecticut," Saxton had grown up around the Gideonites, but, as Rose notes, he "had never been obliged to work with them in the military harness."[81]

However sympathetic he personally might have been, Saxton was surrounded by fellow officers who considered his work on behalf of the Gideonites unimportant and who subjected it to

Major General Rufus Saxton. Courtesy Library of Congress Prints and Photographs Division Washington, DC.

open ridicule. Among his staff, only Captain Edward Hooper, whom Towne declared "the best fellow that ever lived," fully supported Saxton's efforts.[82] Thus, Gannett complained, "Saxton & his staff understand little or nothing of the real wants of the plantation, and though affairs have of course been improved by his presence & authority, very little in proportion to our hopes & our needs has been accomplished." Perhaps reflecting a cultural bias against the military, Gannett contended that instead of Saxton, "We need a civilian, who is a first rate business man,— of force, of fore thought, of devoted interest in this undertaking."[83]

A particular irritation to Saxton came from Brigadier General John Brannan, second-in-command of the Department of the

South, who whenever Hunter was out of the Department would use his temporary authority to "frustrate the abolitionist general in a hundred petty ways." Towne considered Brannan (whom she referred to as "Brennan") "our worst enemy . . . with whom there is no peaceful cooperation."[84] Brannan eventually was removed from the Department, "but not before the confidence of the missionaries in Saxton's ability to withstand the power of the regular military establishment had been seriously weakened."[85]

Saxton complained, "My authority has been questioned by the department commanders, explanations of my official acts have been demanded, those acts annulled, and subordinate officers sustained and encouraged in preventing execution of my orders."[86] He tendered his resignation in frustration but later withdrew it.[87] Some relief came with the passage of the Freedmen's Bureau Act on March 3, 1865. Building on Major General William Sherman's January 16, 1865 Field Order No. 15, which had provided land for black settlement, "abandoned and confiscated" lands now became part of the national domain and the Bureau Act's land clause said that "every male citizen, whether refugee or freedman" was granted occupation of forty acres of land to rent for three years with the possibility of then purchasing the land from the government with "such title as it could convey."[88]

Major General Oliver Howard was appointed to head the Freedmen's Bureau, but he and Saxton soon found themselves torn between the Bureau's commitment to resettle blacks on the coastal islands and President Andrew Johnson's policy of restoring lands to white owners who would pay the taxes they owed, take the oath of allegiance, and obtain a presidential pardon.[89] As Saxton and Howard followed a practice that amounted to obstruction of the president's policy, Johnson hardened his attitude toward the Freedmen's Bureau. Saxton's steady refusal to ignore what he thought had been promised the blacks led to his being replaced by Major General Robert Scott in January 1866. The Freedmen's Bureau also became increasingly subordinate to regular military forces who in late February and early March seized control of restoring lands to their former owners and began forcing the blacks who refused to make labor contracts to leave.[90] As time passed, the Gideonites came to see the

Freedmen's Bureau as being "more interested in securing order and making the freedmen work than in seeing that they went to work under fair conditions."[91]

A Continuing Problem

The Port Royal Experiment was novel in nature and included pioneering activity in many aspects of policy formulation, planning, and cooperation among participants. While such complex operations have become increasingly more common and certain procedures established as routine, modern practitioners are not immune from the same difficulties that plagued their predecessors at Port Royal. Recent U.S. efforts in Iraq, Kosovo, and Somalia have exhibited problems similar to those at Port Royal and illustrate the continued difficulties associated with such activities.

In today's military lexicon, the transition to postcombat operations is called Phase IV, and as at Port Royal, this important aspect of the military art received scant attention when the U.S. invaded Iraq in 2003. Combined Forces Land Component Deputy Commander Lieutenant General William Webster recalled, "Phase IV was always something we were going to get to," and as a result of this inattention, "there was seriously not anything but a skeleton of Phase IV until very late."[92] James Dobbins concludes, "The capacity to look several moves ahead and to understand how interventions will reshape the domestic and external environment of the nations being rebuilt needs to improve."[93]

One of the persistent negative impacts of the failure to thoroughly plan is the forfeiture of Dobbins's "golden hour." This opportunity was threatened in Kosovo where, "as Serbian forces moved out, KLA [the ethnic Albanian Kosovo Liberation Army] elements moved in, seeking to install themselves in positions of authority before the UN Interim Administration in Kosovo (UNMIK) was in a position to assume its new responsibilities fully."[94] A major shortcoming was the slow arrival of UNMIK's civilian police force, which left the ethnic Serb enclaves "subjected to a progression of deadly terrorist-type attacks."[95] Missing the "golden hour" in Kosovo led Dobbins to conclude that "a slow mobilization of civil elements in peace operations can be costly."[96]

Finally, unity of effort remains problematic. The oft-disparaged Gideonites might have taken some comfort in the fact that even today, a certain cultural tension exists between the military and nongovernmental organizations. One observer of the U.S. relief effort in Somalia in the early 1990s opined that "officers simply did not see women in their late twenties with Berkenstock [sic] sandals and 'Save the Whales' T-shirts as experts worthy of consultation."[97] Another noted conversely that "for a variety of reasons, relief agencies tend to be suspicious of military and security personnel, even when they come as peacekeepers."[98]

Every situation is unique, and one must be careful about drawing far-reaching conclusions about experiences particular to a certain set of circumstances. Gerald Knaus, for example, is very critical of what he describes as "the planning school" of nation building theory he attributes to Dobbins.[99] He argues that Dobbins's emphasis on planning and resources suggests "there exists a quantifiable formula for success."[100] Instead, he points out how much is learned during a nation building mission "by trial and error."[101] Yet even Kraus admits his is "an argument for prudence, not recklessness."[102] Since prudence is generally defined as "the ability to recognize and follow the most suitable or sensible course of action; good sense in practical or financial affairs; discretion, circumspection, caution,"[103] it would seem that there is a role for planning, even within Kraus's construct. The Sea Islands' experience certainly provides one scenario for postcombat operations and subsequent developmental efforts that had more in common which the "trial and error" approach of Kraus than the "planning school" of Dobbins. As such it is an instructive case study for present-day would-be nation builders and developers, whatever their theoretical position, who can learn from this episode's challenges with planning and unity of effort—difficulties that unfortunately stubbornly persist.

CHAPTER THREE

A Survey of Philanthropic Society Activity at Port Royal

Lacking a sufficient policy or plan for the Federal occupation of the Sea Islands and the subsequent flight of the white population and abandonment of their slaves, Secretary of the Treasury Salmon Chase dispatched Boston attorney Edward Pierce to Port Royal to assess the situation. Pierce headed south on January 13, 1862, and upon arriving found Reverend Mansfield French was also on the scene conducting his own exploratory visit at the request of the American Missionary Association. Both men agreed on the wisdom of sending missionaries and teachers to assist in the development of the Sea Islands blacks and resolved to generate such support. In a January 19 letter to Chase, Pierce explained the need for such "persons of good sense who could mingle with their religious exhortations advice and counsel as to how these people should act in their new condition, that is, be industrious, orderly, and sober."[1]

Local military commanders agreed with Pierce's assessment and solution. On February 6, Brigadier General Thomas Sherman issued General Order No. 9, in which he stated, "The helpless condition of the blacks inhabiting the vast area in the occupation of the forces of this command calls for immediate action on the part of a highly favored and philanthropic people.... Never was there a nobler or more fitting opportunity for the operation of that considerate and practical benevolence for which the Northern people have ever been distinguished."[2]

Existing religious and abolitionist organizations took up the cause, and in February and March, three new organizations were formed specifically in response to the situation at Port Royal. As a result, an eclectic flood of northern reformers, missionaries, abolitionists, and educators, collectively known as the Gideonites, descended upon the Sea Islands, unleashing what became known as the Port Royal Experiment. Thus, if the U.S. government was "shirking the contraband problem," Laura Roper notes that "minds elsewhere were consciously worrying about it."[3]

In today's vocabulary, such philanthropies would be called "nongovernmental organizations" (NGOs), which, P. J. Simmons boasts, "often make the impossible possible by doing what governments cannot or will not."[4] Certainly, these agencies filled this purpose during the Port Royal Experiment, where the U.S. government had developed only "inadequate and tardy plans."[5] This is not to say, however, that the private organizations did so without friction, tension, and inefficiency. In fact, the variety of agencies associated with the Port Royal Experiment is dizzying. A brief survey of the most influential ones and some observations of the role of these early NGOs on the Sea Islands follows.

Boston Educational Commission

Before he left for his exploratory visit to the Sea Islands, Pierce gained the enthusiastic support of Reverend Jacob Manning, assistant pastor of Old South Church in Boston.[6] In a January 19, 1862, letter from Port Royal to Manning, Pierce confirmed the need of "ministering to these lowest poor children," adding "the compensation and support of such [relief workers] should be derived exclusively from private purses."[7] Manning published Pierce's letter in the January 27 *Boston Transcript* while other prominent Bostonians began sending invitations to a meeting to discuss the matter at Manning's house on February 4.[8] A chairman and secretary were named at this initial meeting, and three days later, a second meeting of seventeen attendees was held at the local Young Man's Christian Association. This group formed the Boston Educational Commission (BEC) and adopted a constitution with the purpose of promoting "the industrial, social, intellectual, moral and religious elevation of persons released from Slavery in the course of the War for the Union." Reflecting the impressive stature of the membership, Massachusetts governor John Andrew was selected to serve as the commission's president.[9]

About two years later, the BEC was reorganized as the New England Freedmen's Aid Society, or simply the New England Society. In both their forms, the Bostonian groups were philanthropic organizations without sectarian or political affiliation. Its noteworthy members included author Edward Everett Hale, economist Edward Atkinson, and engineer Edward Philbrick, who went to Port Royal in 1862 as an agent of the BEC and later served as vice-president of the New England Freedmen's Aid Society.[10]

The cosmopolitan character of these societies attracted a broad range of support from individuals, sewing circles, churches, businesses, and various relief societies. The Bostonians' practice of dispatching traveling agents throughout New England put them in competition with other organizations, especially in Massachusetts, but their aggressive tactics resulted in ninety-six different towns in New England contributing funds and twenty-eight branch societies being in existence in 1865. Each branch society maintained direct communication with an active field worker whose letters provided both information and inspiration for continued philanthropy. Among the Sea Islands teachers supported by the Bostonians was Elizabeth Botume, whose school Edward Whitney financed even after the Freedmen's Aid Society disbanded.[11]

As its name implies, the Boston Educational Commission's greatest work at Port Royal was in the field of education, shunning the expenditure of funds on the alleviation of human wants the Bostonians found excessive in other societies. The New Englanders did not want to relieve the blacks "from the salutary pressure of want" and contrasted this position "with the efforts made by some of our friends in other places."[12]

The Bostonians prided themselves on sending higher quality teachers than the other societies did, but even this select group suffered from a high attrition rate.[13] Of the 72 teachers who went to Port Royal during the first year, 4 died and 32 quit. By January

1864, of the 114 teachers and superintendents sent by the society, 72 remained. A tally made near the end of the war reported that only 54 teachers were present, and of these, 43 had been there less than a year. G. K. Eggleston attributes the heavy turnover to a combination of "climatic conditions, hard work, and lack of adaptability."[14]

The effect of this attrition was compounded by the fact that the BEC's initial focus on the educational needs of the Sea Islands blacks diluted over time. After its reorganization as the New England Freedman's Aid Society (NEFRA), it reported in April 1864 that it had seven teachers at Sea Islands locations and twenty-two elsewhere. This development was a marked change from "our last report [that] our teachers had been at work principally in the South Carolina islands."[15] This expansion of focus away from the BEC's original calling continued when the NEFRA became part of the American Freedmen's Aid Commission on October 20, 1865, and saw itself now as "part of a National Society doing a great national work."[16]

The BEC represents an ad hoc, immediate response to the humanitarian need that developed on the Sea Islands. Its original focus was education. While it no doubt was of Christian character and contained politically active members, it did not conduct itself as a denominational or political advocacy group. It demonstrated competition with other agencies in its fund-raising efforts as well as cooperation with the NEFRA's eventual merger with the American Freedmen's Aid Commission. It changed over time, experiencing both reorganizations and shifting of focus. These changes and the attrition of its teachers combined to dilute its impact on the Sea Islands as the war progressed.

National Freedmen's Relief Association

The National Freedmen's Relief Association (NFRA), which Eggleston considers "the most influential eastern organization," began operating on February 22, 1862, at New York.[17] It grew out of a public meeting called by members of the American Missionary Association (AMA) at Cooper Institute on February 20 to address needs of the Sea Islands blacks as reported by Mansfield French. As a result, the NFRA was formed "to appoint suitable teachers to instruct the Freedmen in industrial and mechanical arts, in the rudiments of education, the principles of Christianity, their accountability to the laws of God and man, their relation to each other as social beings, and all that might be necessary to render them competent to sustain themselves as members of a civilized society."[18]

E. Allen Richardson considers the NFRA "an attempt to broaden the AMA's ability to encompass a variety of ecclesiastical and secular interests," and its work "was intended as a demonstration of free-labor ideology."[19] The free-labor ideology was a complex amalgam that emphasized the value of work in a competitive, free-market economy. It assumed the superiority of northern business practices and saw them as a model for southern economic development.[20] For many free-labor thinkers, the problem facing the former slaves was that slavery had caused the destruction of families and family "instincts," a tendency to lie and steal, and a lack of self-reliance. The free-labor ideology held that these deficiencies could be overcome by education and that the former slaves could be prepared to take their place as free laborers in the competitive marketplace.[21]

For many adherents to the free-labor ideology, there was an "emphasis on the 'freedom' of laborers to contract and the self-discipline of punching a time clock—as opposed to the previous agrarian emphasis on land ownership and the freedom to decide how to husband the land."[22] Thus, by earning wages for their work on large plantations managed by northern whites, the freedmen would benefit morally as well as materially.[23] On the Sea Islands, the prevalence of the free-labor ideology as espoused by the NFRA and others manifested itself in the decision to restore much of the land to its former white owners and to compel the blacks to work under contracts.

The NFRA's philosophical approach to the freedmen was to educate and support them until they were able to provide for themselves, but to offer no additional charity after self-sufficiency had been achieved. Declaring that the former slaves "must be treated as Freemen," the association concluded that "as such they must earn their livelihood, as we do, and not be dependent on charity."[24]

Because its "paramount object" was to promote "self-reliant, self-supporting members of society," the NFRA sought "to discourage the distribution of supplies as free gifts."[25] Instead, NFRA members like Isaac Brinckerhoff advocated self-help, lecturing their charges that "with the enjoyment of a freedman's privileges, comes also a freedman's duties and responsibilities. You cannot get rid of them; they must be met; and unless you are prepared to meet them with a proper spirit, and patiently and cheerfully to fulfill these obligations, you are not worthy of being a freedman."[26]

The National Freedmen's Relief Association was a product of the American Missionary Association, and as such it was different in several ways from the Boston Educational Commission. The NFRA reflected the evangelical influence of the AMA, and its relationship with the AMA was synergistic. Its advocacy of the free-labor ideology and its insistence on self-help served to inform its interpretation of political issues such as land distribution and economic development. Just as the NFRA was an attempt by the AMA to broaden its reach, the NFRA joined the United States Commission for the Relief of the National Freedmen in 1863 in an effort to strengthen its voice in national politics.[27] In both ways, the NFRA reflected the practice of the relief agencies associated with the Port Royal Experiment using organizational strategies to increase their influence.

Port Royal Relief Commission

The Port Royal Relief Commission (PRRC) was organized in Philadelphia on March 20, 1862. Having formed too late to travel to the Sea Islands with the initial wave of the Boston and New York societies, the PRRC dispatched its own contingent on April 8 with a cargo of clothing, as well as representative Laura Towne to oversee the distribution of the items.

Philosophically, the Pennsylvanians often took a middle ground between the ethically based but nonsectarian Bostonians and the evangelical New Yorkers.[28] The PRRC also adopted organizational practices distinct from the other two societies. Confining its efforts to collect materials largely to Philadelphia and its vicinity, it did not form branch societies or employ paid agents. Publicity and donations were generated primarily from its official monthly publication, The *Pennsylvania Freedmen's Bulletin*, and other advertisements and pamphlets. Finally, although its members were dedicated and energetic, its rolls did not include such singularly famous individuals as were found in the other societies.[29]

Much of the initial focus of the PRCC was logistical. Of the $11,582 in cash the PRRC collected in its first year, nearly $5,900 went toward the stocking of a store designed to protect the freedmen "by the fair rates at which the commodities were to be sold, from the exertions of army sutlers and other traders." John Hunn, "a gentleman well qualified for the duty" in part by his previous work with the Underground Railroad in Delaware, ran the store.[30] Hunn's store was so successful that other societies established similar operations using it as an example.[31] Hunn estimated that his fair prices had saved the freedmen some $6,000. The Pennsylvanians were delighted that these savings "much added to the people's ability to buy land for it ought to be known that the blacks at Port Royal are rapidly becoming proprietors of the soil."[32] This encouragement of black land ownership was a hallmark of the PRRC. In a speech titled "The Freedmen of Port Royal," delivered in Philadelphia on November 21, 1864, and then printed in The *Pennsylvania Freedmen's Bulletin*, superintendent Reuben Tomlinson argued, "If there is any class of people in the country who have priority of claim to the confiscated lands of the South, it certainly is that class who have by years of suffering and unrequited toil given to these lands any value they may now possess."[33]

Soon the PRRC determined that "the immediate [physical] demands of the people" had been met, and so the Pennsylvanians resolved to "next turn their attention to the necessity of industrial organization, and the means needed for the people's moral and intellectual development."[34] This goal, according to Willie Lee Rose, was an attempt to teach the Sea Islanders "the rudimentary arts of civilized life" and "to instruct them in the elements of an English education and the simple truths of the Bible divested as much as possible of all sectarian bias."[35] Pursuant to this object, the PRRC sent several teachers to South Carolina, "but their work was never pushed."[36] Instead, the Pennsylvanians soon boldly declared the work of the relief societies on the Sea Islands "in all respects an absolute success" and the fifteen thousand freed blacks there to be "self-supporting."[37] Based on this assumption and endeavoring to meet new demands created by Federal Army advances elsewhere "in the southwest especially, where the number of liberated blacks had reached a figure somewhere between one and two thousand," the Pennsylvanians "determined to enlarge their field of action."[38] Reflecting this broadened scope, the PRRC officially became the Pennsylvania Freedmen's Relief Association (PFRA) in October 1863, and the organization's educational focus soon shifted to Washington and its immediate vicinity, Virginia, and Tennessee.[39] One consequence of this decision was the reduced influence on the Sea Islands of the relief organization that had been perhaps most sympathetic to black land ownership.

In spite of the PRRC's eventual emphasis elsewhere, the teacher most famously associated with the Port Royal Experiment, Laura Towne, was commissioned by that organization and eventually became superintendent of the Philadelphia schools on the Sea Islands.[40] Towne headed south with the initial PRCC shipment in 1862, and she ran the famous Penn School on St. Helena Island until her death in 1901. She began her classes on September 22 in the Brick Church, a Baptist building built shortly before the war, but the elders grew uncomfortable with an independent school on their premises. In response, the PFRA purchased a three-room, prefabricated schoolhouse and shipped it south in sections in October 1864. In early 1865, Towne proudly shifted her operation to the new building.[41] As a testimony to her dedication to helping the Sea Island blacks, Pierce declared Towne "the best illustration of permanence and perseverance" he had ever known.[42] Unfortunately, such resiliency was the exception rather than the rule among the Gideonites.

Of the three relief agencies specifically formed in response to the situation which developed after the Federal seizure of Port Royal, the Pennsylvania group was arguably the one most sincerely devoted to the innate welfare of the Sea Islands black population and most free from internal agenda. Its systematic and deliberate shift from immediate humanitarian relief to education reflects the phased operational sequencing of many relief efforts. Its tendency to declare success points to the need of organizations to use quantifiable "measures of effectiveness" to inform and support such assertions. This assumed mission accomplishment encouraged the Pennsylvanians to focus elsewhere and contributed to a dilution and attrition of still-needed effort on the Sea Islands.

American Freedmen's Union Commission

As the Civil War progressed, the various organizations devoted to assisting the freedmen gravitated into two distinct groups. The more liberal group included the secular and Quaker societies, while the missionary organizations constituted a more conservative group. Although initial enthusiasm helped "enforce a grudging cooperation," competition and quarreling among the groups often frustrated progress.[43] In an effort to create a stronger, more unified voice in national politics, in 1863 five major secular groups (the New England Freedmen's Aid Society, the National Freedmen's Relief Association of New York, the Pennsylvania Freedmen's Relief Association, the Cincinnati-based Western Freedmen's Aid Commission, and the Chicago-based Northwestern Freedmen's Aid Commission) joined forces to create the United States Commission for the Relief of the National Freedmen (USCRNF).[44]

The merger represented incremental progress, but it did not settle the matter. Nina Mjagkij calls the USCRNF "simply a paper organization with no officers and no coordinating authority."[45] Fund-raising competition continued to hinder unity of effort, and a second cooperative attempt was made in February 1865 when the Pennsylvania and New York societies joined with the Baltimore Association for the Moral and Educational Improvement of the Colored People to create the American Freedmen's Aid Union (AFUA).

In May, after the resignations of officers who were also members of the American Missionary Association, the New York National Freedmen's Relief Association joined the AFUA. When the Western Freedmen's Aid Commission, the Northwestern Freedmen's Aid Commission, and the Freedmen's Aid Commission of Western Pennsylvania joined in August 1865, the expanded organization took on the name of the American Freedmen's Aid Commission (AFAC). In spite of any previous differences, the various member groups now were united in large measure by the cause of black suffrage.[46]

In a further effort to broaden its base, the AFAC began discussions with the American Union Commission (AUC), an organization that had been organized in mid-1864 and focused its efforts primarily on white refugees in the South who had suffered because of their Union sympathies. Major General Oliver Howard, head of the Bureau of Refugees, Freedmen, and Abandoned Lands (popularly called the Freedmen's Bureau), participated in much of the planning and throughout the process was in contact with the leaders of all secular and denominational organizations involved in relief or educational work in the South. The efforts paid off on January 31, 1866, when the AFAC and the AUC united to form the American Freedmen's and Union Commission or, more simply, the American Freedmen's Union Commission (AUFC).[47] The AFUC was intended to be a biracial organization that James Miller McKim claimed would ignore "all distinctions of race or color." The result, McKim hoped, would be an organization "broader and stronger" than an organization focused on the former slaves alone.[48]

This nobly intended goal had the unintended consequence of alienating many contributors to the freedmen's cause who objected to including southern whites in their charity.[49] Others, including Laura Towne at St. Helena, were suspicious of the Freedmen's Bureau's relationship with the AFUC and the impact it might have on the autonomy of local efforts. "When you get this great organization in working order," Towne wrote McKim, "is it your intention to put it under the patronage of the President: that is, merge it into a new political power called an educational Bureau?"[50]

Like the other organizations discussed so far, the American Freedmen's Union Commission changed and evolved over the course of several years. Such structural development is a reminder that even philanthropic organizations are bureaucracies and experience all the strengths and weaknesses inherent in such a status. Umbrella organizations no doubt increase the collective voice of their members, but they may do so at the cost of their members' individual voices. As the organization expands to embrace the common denominator, specific interests are marginalized, such as whether the AFUC's focus should have been on needy blacks or whites or both. Likewise, as the organization grows in size, it may become less agile and responsive at the tactical level such as Towne feared.

American Missionary Association

The American Missionary Association (AMA) was founded in 1846 in Buffalo, New York, with the initial focus of establishing Christian missions around the world. From its inception, the AMA was strongly against slavery and considered the Gospel to be a powerful abolitionist weapon.[51] In many ways, the AMA occupied the important antislavery middle ground between the Garrisonian demand for immediate, universal reform and the older church mission boards that were often dominated by men willing to be more accommodating to slaveholding. The AMA represented a decidedly antislavery yet practical approach.[52]

The AMA's understanding of education as an important avenue for black advancement was demonstrated by its establishment of Berea College in Kentucky in 1859, and with the opportunities created by the Civil War, the AMA "felt itself specially called for and providentially equipped for . . . the instruction and elevation of the colored people."[53] For the evangelical AMA, religion and education were inseparable. "Christian schools," it declared, "know absolutely nothing of education which does not magnify the Bible and keep it foremost."[54] Armed with this philosophical approach, the AMA quickly withdrew its missionary efforts elsewhere and "concentrated its energies upon this new field in the South."[55] The AMA dispatched the Reverend L. C. Lockwood to Hampton, Virginia, which led to the founding of the "first day-school for the Freedmen" on September 17, 1861, under the direction of Mary Peake.[56] It was also at the request of prominent AMA members Lewis Tappan and George Whipple that the Reverend Mansfield French was sent to the Sea Islands to determine what contribution the New York area could make there.[57]

The scope of the situation on the Sea Islands as reported by French gave the pragmatic AMA pause, and it feared the dire conditions exceeded its existing capabilities. Tappan and Whipple concluded that "the emergency required some further instrumentalists," which would be "likely to enlist a constituency that the Association could not reach."[58] To address this issue, they called a public meeting at Cooper Institute on February 20. As a result, the National Freedmen's Relief Association (NFRA) was formed on February 22. Even though the NFRA was a distinct organization from the AMA, the ties remained strong. French, for example, although an officer of the NFRA, continued to send reports to Whipple at the AMA.[59]

In addition to giving impetus to the NFRA, by 1863 the AMA was also sending its own representatives directly into the field. These missionaries maintained a strong evangelical fervor and a desire to transform the freedmen. W. J. Richardson, the AMA representative in Beaufort, considered that "the great work is to unlearn them and learn them from, the vices, habits, and associations of their former lives."[60] Such a statement reflected the free-labor ideology that was prevalent in the AMA.[61]

The AMA saw the creation of the Freedmen's Bureau in 1865 as a welcome mechanism for focusing its free-labor initiatives. According to E. Allen Richardson, the resulting relationship was "unique, for in no other instance was power so completely integrated between church and state in a complex, symbiotic pattern of dual appointments, mutual agendas, and shared perceptions about the nature of Reconstruction."[62] The AMA's ties with both the NFRA and the Freedmen's Bureau helped ensure the dominance of the free-labor ideology in the Port Royal Experiment.

This influence was magnified because the sheer size of the AMA gave it an advantage over other societies in terms of both personnel and financial support. By 1866, it had fielded a force of 327 teachers on the Sea Islands. By comparison, the PFRA was supporting just 60.[63] More importantly, as a variety of forces conspired to reduce the efforts of other organizations, the AMA continued to labor on behalf of the freedmen, its work including support for the Avery Institute in Charleston, which served as a training ground for many of South Carolina's low-country teachers.[64]

Unlike the other organizations, the American Missionary Association was in existence at the time of the seizure of Port Royal. Its head start, infrastructure, size, and connections gave it considerable influence and economies of scale, especially in promoting its belief in the free-labor ideology and being able to sustain a longevity that eluded other organizations. While it had a proven record in the field of education, as its name would suggest, the AMA was at its core evangelical. As such, its close relationship with the government's Freedmen's Bureau would certainly elicit discussion in today's environment that it did not in the 1860s.

Threads of Continuity

Although the work of the various private-sector agencies on the Sea Islands was imperfect, it was nonetheless remarkable. Stepping into a "limbo between the old and new," they collectively filled a void and brought some order to what otherwise would have been complete confusion.[65] From this brief survey of the participants, it is possible to draw some broad observations of enduring relevance, particularly to the efforts of modern-day NGOs. These include issues of agendas, competition, size, donor fatigue, and impact.

In his study of the diplomatic changes after the Cold War, David Davenport comments on the ability of NGOs to act as

"special-interest groups that would sacrifice a wide range of other
... values to pursue their own agenda."[66] The NFRA's devotion to
the free-labor ideology and its evangelical zeal are examples of
agendas as part of a philanthropic effort. Likewise, Simmons's
caution that NGOs may "lapse into old-fashioned interest group
politics that produces gridlock" was borne out in fund-raising
competition among the Sea Islands philanthropies.[67]

In his study of Iraq and Afghanistan, Francis Fukuyama
finds "a veritable swarm of nongovernmental organizations."
The result is that "many of the programs are duplicative, do not
respond to local needs, and are sometimes at cross purposes with
one another."[68] Such competition seems to have developed also
at Port Royal, where Rose concludes "there were too many chiefs
and too few Indians" and "everybody wanted the leading part
in conducting the freedmen to the promised land."[69] The result
as described by C. Vann Woodward was that "organized groups
struggled against each other for the allegiance of the slaves, the
support of the military, and the backing of Washington authorities."[70] In such an environment, the Gideonite who found "friction in every quarter—-military, religious, and political" should
come as no surprise.[71]

In a study of NGOs operating in India in the late 1990s, Peter
Uvin, Pankaj Jain, and L. David Brown identify "quantitative scaling up" or becoming larger in size as a way NGOs can increase
their impact.[72] The broad direct and indirect influence of the
AMA on the Sea Islands certainly was a function of its large size.
Conversely, the smaller organizations like the PFRA had less
influence.

In their study of the 2004 tsumani triggered by the Sumatra-
Andaman earthquake, Philip Brown and Jessica Minty find evidence of donor fatigue, which they describe as "a state in which
donors have already exhausted their resources or in which they
grow complacent about appeals for charitable gifts, leading to a
diminished public response."[73] Donor fatigue also plagued the
Port Royal Experiment, where by 1870, Laura Towne lamented,
"our school exists on charity, and charity that is weary."[74] The
steady attrition of the Boston Educational Commission's teachers is a related phenomenon.

In spite of these challenges, there is no doubt that NGOs make a difference. Even hard-bitten military commanders such as Major General S. L. Arnold considered the NGOs in Somalia to be "the real heroes of this operation."[75] Elizabeth Ware Pearson expresses a similar sentiment in declaring, "There was a good deal of courage in what [the Gideonites] did."[76] While most historians assess the Port Royal Experiment as at best a mixed success, there is no doubt that the various philanthropies relieved suffering, advanced education, and met humanitarian needs that otherwise would have been neglected. What is more, Rose argues that "by May of 1865 the aid societies, acting independently but cooperatively, had already accomplished their most important work. For they had served as gadflies to awaken the Administration and Congress to belated action to meet the impending social crisis."[77]

If this brief survey reveals anything, it is that while collectively lumped together as the "Gideonites," the character of the group was far from monolithic. Each agency was unique in its approach, execution, and development, but in its own way, each made a contribution. Today's NGOs continue to meet similar challenges that their predecessors encountered on the Sea Islands and continue to do yeoman's work. They can be justifiably proud to share a legacy with the philanthropic relief agencies of the Port Royal Experiment.

CHAPTER FOUR

Development's Different Meanings to Developers and Stakeholders

Among the numerous definitions and connotations of the term development, one common theme is that development encompasses "change" in a variety of aspects of the human condition.[1] Robert Chambers notes that the preference is for "good change," but because "any development agenda is value-laden," interpretations of what "good change" is are also problematic.[2] As Ravi Kanbur observes, "Since [development] depend[s] on values and on alternative conceptions of the good life, there is no uniform or unique answer."[3] Lynnell Simonson and Virginia Bushaw point out that even a seemingly innocuous needs assessment is "by definition, a value judgment comparing the current state of affairs with some more desirable conditions."[4] In part because of these difficulties, developers, even as they seek to "do good," run the risk of "intervening in the lives of others without understanding the objectives and value systems" of those they are intending to help.[5] Such was the case with the Port Royal Experiment when a diverse group of actors flocked to the Sea Islands, all with their own vision of how best to deal with the new reality of some ten thousand now masterless slaves.[6]

The varied nature of these developers created a host of different agendas and motivations. What they had in common was that they were white and had been drawn to the Sea Islands by the condition resulting from the sudden creation of a free black population. Where they differed was in how they responded to the freedmen, and historian Eric Foner contends that "each group had its own ideas about how the transition to freedom should take place."[7]

As these developers attempted to change life on the Sea Islands, their own agendas consciously or unconsciously affected their actions, sometimes to the detriment of the local population. Such a phenomenon is consistent with Francis Fukuyama's observation that "agent incentives can never be fully aligned with the interests of their principals."[8] Caught up in their own perspective of the moment, many of the developers seem to have paid little attention to the former slaves' thoughts on what "good change" meant to them.

Subsequent historians have debated the overall applicability of Willie Lee Rose's declaration of the Port Royal Experiment as a "Rehearsal for Reconstruction," noting for example that this particular transition from slave to free labor was uniquely affected by the absence of the former white masters. Even such critics, however, admit the Sea Islands experience provides a useful revelation of "Northern intentions and black desires."[9] As such, it serves as an enlightening case study of one of the many difficulties facing developers and suggests the participatory approach to development may help mitigate this particular challenge.

The Gideonites and the Free-Labor Ideology

Perhaps the most visible presence among the Sea Islands developers was the host of teachers and missionaries known collectively as the Gideonites. This group consisted largely of young New England men freshly graduated from Harvard, Yale, or divinity school and young women with backgrounds as teachers or members of the abolitionist movement.[10]

As a group, the Gideonites held a fervent belief in the free-labor ideology. In their minds, the problem facing the former slaves was that slavery had caused the destruction of families and family "instincts," a tendency to lie and steal, and a lack of self-reliance. The free-labor ideology held that these deficiencies could be overcome by education and that the former slaves could be prepared to take their place as free laborers in the competitive marketplace.[11] For the Gideonites, free-labor ideology became "the starting point for discussions of the postwar South."[12]

Along with the free-labor ideology, a new philosophy of "self-ownership" rather than "land ownership" had been steadily gaining traction in the North. This notion put "emphasis on the 'freedom' of laborers to contract and the self-discipline of punching a time clock—as opposed to the previous agrarian emphasis on land ownership and the freedom to decide how to husband the land."[13] Thus, by earning wages for their work on large plantations managed by northern whites, the freedmen would benefit morally as well as materially. It would be this understanding of freedom that would drive the efforts of Gideonites like Edward Philbrick, who would ultimately be the principal land and labor overseer of the Port Royal Experiment.[14]

The Freedmen's Vision of Land Ownership

The Gideonites were convinced of the moral and economic superiority of their native North, and they wholeheartedly expected the Sea Islands blacks to embrace enthusiastically the free-labor ideology. But instead of being willing to "work the cotton plantations as wage laborers and learn the importance of efficiency and attending to market forces," the former slaves quickly showed they had a completely different vision of their future.[15] For them, cotton was inexorably tied to slavery and working for a master rather than themselves. Instead, the Sea Islands blacks understood freedom as owning their own land, farming it as they pleased, and living largely independent of the marketplace.[16] Many Gideonites feared such a notion of freedom would lead only "to idle and thriftless habits."[17] In cases of such dichotomy, Andrew Natsios, former administrator of the U.S. Agency for International Development, contends, "development initiatives must meet the country's needs and its people's problems as they perceive them, not as distant policymakers imagine them."[18] The Port Royal Experiment was not immune from this tension, and from its start, it was marked by conflicting views and interests among its participants.

In an effort to gain an understanding of the situation and develop a plan, Secretary of the Treasury Salmon Chase dispatched Boston lawyer Edward Pierce to Port Royal in January 1862. While Pierce noted some freedmen "wanted a white man for a 'protector,'" they still "would like to be free."[19] For these Sea Islands blacks, "to be free," according to Foner, meant being able "to take control of the conditions under which they labored, free themselves from subordination to white authority, and carve out the greatest measure of economic autonomy."[20] Critical to this notion of freedom was land ownership.

Martin Abbott summarizes, "As one of their most cherished dreams, the great majority of ex-slaves longed for ownership of the soil; to them 'forty acres and a mule' symbolized the essence of liberty."[21] Pierce recognized this desire for land and saw its merits. He proposed the freedmen "should have the power to acquire the fee simple of land, either with the proceeds of their labor or as a reward of special merit; and it would be well to quicken their zeal for good behavior by proper recognitions."[22] Instead, after much debate and many changes in policy, the land was confiscated by the U.S. government for nonpayment of taxes and sold by and large to whites. Most Sea Islanders viewed this development as a betrayal, a sentiment Rose concludes "the Northerners understood but did not view with sufficient sympathy."[23]

Self-Interest

The fluid environment on the Sea Islands was ripe for exploitation. Pierce noted early on that "no man, not even the best of men, charged with the duties which ought to belong to the guardians of these people, should be put in a position where there would be such a conflict between his humanity and self-interest."[24] Unfortunately, Pierce's fear came to fruition.

The developers that came to the Sea Islands were northerners, and they understandably were influenced by how their actions in South Carolina would impact their native region. One of the early arrivals was cotton agent Lieutenant Colonel William Reynolds, who had "for many years occupied the most prominent position in the cotton trade" and was well-connected to that activity in Rhode Island.[25] Reflecting this influence, Reynolds developed a plan to collect cotton that would then be shipped to New York for ginning. Pierce objected to this procedure in part because it would increase employment in the North but leave the Sea Islands blacks wanting. It quickly became apparent to Pierce that the rapid collection and shipment of cotton was Reynolds's "controlling consideration," while Pierce thought the black population should be the principal concern.[26]

While Reynolds's approach was designed to benefit the North at the exclusion of the Sea Islanders, other developers championed a more synergistic tactic that still reflected their regional concerns. Pennsylvanian James McKim saw the Port Royal freedmen as "ten thousand new customers." If the black population could be transitioned to productive wage earners, they would soon demand "pots, kettles, pans, brushes, brooms, knives, forks, spoons, soap, candles, combs, Yankee clocks, etc. etc" which could be provided by northern manufacture. A staunch abolitionist, McKim could recognize "an overwhelming economical argument" for freedom as well as the obvious moral one.[27] Gideonite Austa French concurred, writing, "Imagine the trade set in motion the moment they get wages. What a brisk market for everything conceivable."[28] McKim and French wanted the lives of the Sea Island blacks to improve, but they could not help but also notice the northern economic benefits of such development.

Rather than raising cotton, many freedmen preferred to grow vegetables and sell fish to the soldiers. Economists such as Edward Atkinson argued that instead the blacks should focus on cotton and buy western grains.[29] Rose concludes, "Their vision of a freed people as agricultural peasants devoted to a single-crop economy and educated to a taste for consumer goods supplied by Northern factories fulfills the classic pattern of tributary economies the world over." The result was an ambiguous "philanthropic-commercial venture" that resulted in many "planter-missionaries [that] were pure economic imperialists."[30]

The greatest conflict of interest occurred with the sale of the land abandoned by the southern whites. While most Gideonites felt the freedmen were "entitled to some preference in the disposition of the lands whereon they had toiled so long without recompense," staunch free-labor adherents such as Philbrick pointed to the dangers of government involvement and advocated private ownership, so long as the new owners were not selfishly motivated.[31] John Murray Forbes, with whom Philbrick had organized a consortium, argued that the danger of "speculators" could best be avoided by "combinations of liberal men at the North, whose chief concern would be to give the experiment a fair trial under the system of both free labor and the stimulus of individual interest."[32]

To the chagrin of many missionaries, such arguments carried the day, and when the first land sales occurred on March 9, 1863, Philbrick and his joint-stock company bought eleven cotton plantations, totaling eight thousand acres, and leased two others from the government. For a mere seven thousand dollars, Philbrick and his partners had gained possession of one-third of St. Helena Island and indirect control over the nearly one thousand people who lived there.[33]

Missionaries immediately became suspicious of Philbrick's intentions. Reuben Tomlinson sarcastically referred to "E. S. Philbrick, 'the Philanthropist.'"[34] Laura Towne counseled freedmen not to trust Philbrick.[35] The criticism intensified after Philbrick's first year of management proved successful. Mansfield French concluded that Philbrick and other investors were "getting rich by the labor of the blacks, and while they were lining their pockets, their laborers were no richer at the end of the year than they were at the beginning."[36] William Gannett, who left his teaching position to become a plantation superintendent for Pierce, noted painfully that he and Philbrick were viewed with askance. "Did you know we had long ceased to be philanthropists or even Gideonites?," he wrote. "We are nothing now but speculators, and the righteous rail against us."[37] "We have little reputation," he confessed "except for prosperous selfishness."[38]

One of Gannett's friends asked him "if you consider yourself now as a missionary or a raiser of cotton," cautioning Gannett he "will very likely to be drawn into business life, for I think the emancipation business must grow in a commercial character."[39] Such a perception troubled Gannett, who was pure in intent and embarrassed "to find philanthropy paying so well." To preclude any future conflict of interest, he caused his contract with Philbrick for the 1864 crop to be rewritten so that Gannett could earn no less than one thousand but no more than four thousand dollars. He also used his earnings to establish a Pine Grove Fund and kept a teacher at St. Helena Island for several years.[40]

Philbrick had no such reservations about his profits. Towne originally had understood it was Philbrick's intention eventually to sell his land to the freedmen at cost, but he instead decided to keep his property. Towne reported Philbrick felt, "It will not be well for them . . . to make money so fast on their cotton and land as they would now." He steadfastly argued that it was in the freedmen's best interest to practice self-help and to be constantly striving for an improved life. Towne took the opposing view, wondering "if it is good for [Philbrick] to be getting rich so fast?"[41] Even Philbrick acknowledged the temptation, confessing "it may be difficult to fathom one's own motives in such cases." From the point of view of the freedmen, however, Rose believes the issue was much clearer. For them, Philbrick was "the embodiment of a man whose good motives had been corrupted by good fortune."[42] He was among the "pompous men who had the folly to identify their own economic advantage with the truest philanthropy."[43]

The Participatory Approach

The competing visions of "good change" found the Port Royal Experiment "caught between African Americans' desires to own their homelands, on which they expected to operate a sustainable subsistence economy, and Northern capitalists' visions of freed people's cheap wage labor on white-controlled commercial plantations, with the prospects of trickle-down prosperity and education for citizenship."[44] The economic opportunists notwithstanding, many Gideonites wanted what they genuinely believed was best for the Sea Islanders. However, even these pure-intentioned developers paid insufficient attention to what the Sea Islanders sought for themselves. In the absence of strong freedmen commitment to the developmental plan, the result was at best mixed success.

The tension between the Gideonites' and the freedmen's perspectives might have been reduced had the Gideonites practiced more of a participatory approach in their efforts. This technique "assumes that societal groups have conflicting interests, and focuses on empowering oppressed groups to transform social structures into more equitable societies."[45] It requires consultation with the groups that are likely to be affected by the developmental effort, considering them to be "stakeholders" capable of making a positive contribution to the effort and enhancing its likelihood of success rather than mere objects of programs and policies determined by others. Andy Sumner and Michael Tribe argue that "the more sensitive a project, program, or policy is to stakeholder interests, particularly at a community level, the more likely is the participatory approach to reap dividends in the form of effective design, implementation, and operation."[46] Similarly, Simonson and Bushaw point to the legitimacy that community involvement bestows on proposed solutions.[47] Specifically addressing the contentious issue of land reform, Solon Barraclough observes that this process "necessarily requires participation by its intended beneficiaries as well as by the large holders, who lose some of their land rights, and by the state that, as a minimum, provides the legal framework for reform."[48]

One of the best examples of the effectiveness of the participatory approach to development is the Marshall Plan. In outlining his proposal during his Harvard commencement address in 1947, Secretary of State George Marshall insisted, "It would be neither fitting nor efficacious for this Government to undertake to draw up unilaterally a program designed to place Europe on its feet economically. This is the business of the Europeans. The initiative, I think, must come from Europe. The role of this country should consist of friendly aid in the drafting of a European program and of later support of such a program so far as it may be practical for us to do so."[49] Natsios agrees that when it comes to reconstruction, "a country must drive its own development needs and priorities. The role of donor organizations is to support and assist this process as partners toward a common objective."[50] Jeremi Suri adds that "nation building can work only when the people own it."[51] As Suri and Natsios would suggest, the Marshall Plan was widely successful, while the competing Soviet program, which lacked this participatory component, was not.

On a much smaller scale than the Marshall Plan, the non-governmental organization Oxfam America has used a similar strategy to develop a "project partners" model that relies on local communities to determine their own needs and carry out development projects.[52] Various methods can be used to accomplish the consultation required by this participatory approach, including meetings with influential community leaders, grass-roots forums, surveys, and focus groups.[53] Although at first blush such techniques may seem anachronistic to the situation on the Sea Islands, in fact many opportunities existed to accomplish their intent.

As Pierce surveyed the conditions at Port Royal, he identified several potential avenues for a participatory approach and seemed to imply some appreciation of its value. He made a concerted effort to visit the area plantations and have "familiar conversations . . . with several laborers, more or less, as time permitted—sometimes inquiries made of them, as they collected in groups, *as to what they desired us to do with and for them* " (emphasis added).[54] In spite of this assertion, by and large, Pierce's interests lay with gathering technical information about the agricultural cycle, the labor system, and economic conditions. Rather than genuinely seeking participatory input, Pierce was merely pursuing the traditional professional expert model to "gather quantitative data from the community under study, analyze it, and report the strengths and deficiencies of the community, and possibly a solution to the problems identified."[55] There is little in Pierce's report to indicate he regarded the freedmen as genuine stakeholders in the process of developing the system under which they would come to live. Qualifiers to his method of inquiry such as "more or less," "as time permitted," and "sometimes" clearly indicate the cursory nature of Pierce's efforts to determine the freedmen's perspective of their future. Indeed, at the same time Pierce made his minor inquiries, he also made it a point to impress upon his audience reasons why "it was for their interest" that they "pursue the course of sobriety and industry" that the government was preparing to present. [56]

Had Pierce chosen to pursue more aggressively the participatory approach, he would have found a variety of likely sources with which to consult. While issues with literacy and other administrative and logistical concerns obviously rendered the survey technique impossible, Pierce still had access to community leaders, grassroots forums, and focus groups.

As Pierce made his rounds, he noted the presence of individuals "more intelligent than the average, such as the carpenter, the plowman, [and] the religious leader."[57] He singled out boat pilots as holding a particularly "delicate and responsible position, involving honesty and skill."[58] There was even a black cabinetmaker who for several years had been secretly holding night classes for slaves.[59] Pierce found that such exceptional individuals occupied "recognized positions among their fellows, either by virtue of superior knowledge or devotion." As such, these community leaders represented a valuable voice in articulating the freedmen's interests. Pierce, however, did not view this segment of the population in that light. Instead, he saw them as a tool that "when properly approached by us, may be expected to have a beneficial influence on the more ignorant, and help to create that public opinion in favor of good conduct which, among the humblest as among the highest, is most useful."[60] Pierce had seemingly already defined for the freedmen what was "good conduct" and had adopted a manipulative and pragmatic approach to his own understanding of what was "useful" rather than empowering the existing community leadership to represent local interests.

Pierce was very conscious in pursuing what he considered "a part of my duty to attend some of their religious meetings, and learn further about these people what could be derived from such a source."[61] This venue afforded Pierce a perfect chance for a grassroots forum to determine the freedmen's interests if he opted to treat it as such. Pierce took such opportunities to counsel the freedmen that President Abraham Lincoln "was thinking what he could do for them," but Pierce apparently did not avail himself of this opportunity to solicit the assembly's ideas of what help they might desire for themselves.[62] Instead, Pierce's contention was always that the Sea Islands blacks would perform "with proper motives set before them," but his assumption seems to have been consistently that those motives would come from the outsiders rather than the freedmen.[63]

Much of the supervision of the antebellum work on the Sea Islands plantations was entrusted to a black driver whose duties and position Pierce equated to a foreman on a northern farm. Pierce determined the drivers to be men of "considerable judgment and knowledge of plantation economy" and acknowledged that with the departure of the white population, the driver maintained diminished but still noteworthy authority. He concluded the drivers, "when properly advised and controlled, may be made available in securing the productiveness of the plantations and the good of the laborers."[64] While the drivers "were found very ready to answer inquiries and communicate all information," Pierce treated them primarily as a means to a largely predetermined end rather than a voice in determining the nature of that end.[65] Philbrick envisioned the driver as being pivotal in transitioning to the new order, and clearly the assembly of drivers represented the equivalent of a modern-day focus group whose ideas and reactions could be used to help gauge the black population's interests.[66] Focus groups are especially valuable in the participatory approach because of their ability to "stimulate discussions in which one group member reacts to comments made by another." The result is a "synergistic group effect."[67] Pierce did not optimize this resource for that purpose, instead using a much more directed dialogue.

Federal authorities eventually tapped into the indigenous black leadership on January 12, 1865, when Secretary of War Edwin Stanton assembled a group of twenty ministers, barbers, pilots, sailors, and former drivers and "asked their opinion on a dozen problems involving their welfare."[68] This approach created friction with Major General William Sherman when Stanton met with the assembly privately to investigate rumors of Sherman's "almost criminal dislike" of blacks. Although the former slaves gave Sherman high praise, he was still indignant "that the great

War Secretary should have catechized negroes concerning the character of a general who had commanded a hundred thousand men in battle, had captured cities, conducted sixty-five thousand men successfully across four hundred miles of hostile territory, and had just brought tens of thousands of freedmen to a place of security."[69] Sherman's perception of being second-guessed represents one challenge to practitioners of the participatory approach.

Nonetheless, after these meetings, Sherman issued his famous Special Field Order No. 15, which set aside a reserve of land for black settlement. Although Sherman's motivations were largely based on military expediency, LaWanda Cox credits this order with having a "direct origin in the desires of the Negroes."[70] Indeed, when asked how they could best care for themselves and aid the government in maintaining their freedom, the spokesman for the freedmen whom Stanton had queried replied, "The way we can best take care of ourselves is to have land, and turn it and till it by our own labor."[71] Stanton reportedly boasted that this was the first time in the history of the nation that government officials had gone to the blacks and asked them what they wanted for themselves.[72]

Such self-assessment notwithstanding, others felt that Stanton, like Pierce, did not take full advantage of the freedmen's input. Major General Oliver Howard in particular felt Stanton did not carry the information back to Washington to share with other policy makers, lamenting that "it would have been wise if our statesmen could have received, digested and acted upon the answers these men gave to their questions."[73] Indeed, as head of the Freedman's Bureau, Howard remembered this lesson and, while laboring against myriad overwhelming challenges, nonetheless used the participatory approach to help gather stakeholder input into thorny issues such as the disposition of land.[74]

The area in which the Gideonites most seemed to acknowledge and act on the freedmen's desires was education. Pierce reports, "All of proper age, when inquired of, expressed a desire to have their children taught to read and write, and to learn themselves."[75] Missionary and teacher Elizabeth Botume was told by one black woman, "Us wants to larn, fur we've been in darkness too long, an' now we're in light, us wants to larn."[76] Another former slave told William Gannett that as far as education was concerned, "We pant for it, sir."[77] In the area of education, the Gideonites satisfied Natsios's requirement that "development initiatives must meet the country's needs and its people's problems as they perceive them, not as distant policymakers imagine them."[78]

Of course, this educational advancement coincided with the free-labor ideology espoused by the Gideonites, so their zeal in this area cannot be attributed fully to the participatory approach. Still, the Sea Islands blacks willingly embraced this aspect of the Port Royal Experiment like they did no other. When Laura Towne and Ellen Murray began the Penn School on September 22, 1862, 41 students were enrolled. Three days later, that number had jumped to 76, and by January 1863 there were more than 150 students.[79] Enrollment soon neared 200, and by the 1870s, Towne and Murray were compelled to turn away all but the most promising students.[80] Rose considers education "the most successful branch of the experiment" and notes that "where the superintendents met stubborn and passive resistance, the teachers were joyfully accepted everywhere."[81] Even if not by conscious Gideonite design, the educational activities associated with the Port Royal Experiment suggest the value of the participatory approach to development.

Implications for Development

The inherent value-laden nature of development continues to present problems for recent nation building efforts. David Tucker notes that

> Modernization theory assumes that the logic of economic development produces modern, democratic, prosperous nations. Indeed, we seem often to have assumed that history would replicate around the world versions of the United States. This assumption is unfounded or, rather, founded on a false universalism. Our ideal of a "wealthy, equitable, democratic, stable, and autonomous" society, like the notion of development itself, is not indigenous

to most of the world, which may conceive of the good society as one that is "simple, austere, hierarchical, authoritarian, disciplined, and martial." Our efforts to build a nation, a good society as we conceive it, may founder because our image of the good society "may not constitute a meaningful model or reference" for those we are assisting.

The result is "our principles, our notions of what a good society is, are not necessarily in agreement with theirs . . . [which] explains why they resist our efforts."[82]

The intentions of most of the Gideonites were undoubtedly humanitarian, and some like Pierce even demonstrated some effort to consult with the freedmen. Certainly, the Gideonites' educational programs met a stated desire of the freedmen, but as Ilan Kapoor notes, developers consistently tend to be more participatory in educational programs than in political or economic ones.[83] In these latter areas, the participatory approach that was practiced on the Sea Islands was of the sort Jonathan Pugh cautions is "often used to implement the vision of the elites, rather than let that vision organically develop through an emerging sense of aspiration from within the general population around real material concerns for development."[84] In his study of development in St. Lucia after the eastern Caribbean island gained its independence from Britain in 1979, Pugh finds evidence of a mentality that "certain elites are best placed to take over the management of land." Therefore, the local population has a duty to, and presumably is best served by, "handing over of responsibility to those who know better."[85] Such an approach, former U.S. national security advisor Anthony Lake cautions, amounts to "dangerous hubris." Instead, he recommends an approach whereby "we . . . help nations build themselves."[86] Unfortunately, a decidedly more elitist approach to development unfolded on the Sea Islands.

The result was that the stakeholders in the process did not take ownership of it, violating what Natsios considers "the first . . . and perhaps the most important" principle of development.[87] Rather than embracing the economic developmental program, many of the Sea Islanders actively resisted it by sabotaging cotton production, filing grievances with federal government authorities, and demanding more pay.[88] On the other hand, they showed their approval for the education program in which they had been more active participants by agreeing to pay a tax to support the schools.[89] The participatory approach is not a panacea. Simonson and Bushaw correctly note it is "easier said than done," and Natsios admits "nurturing country ownership is a laborious process that emerges with time and effort."[90] Nonetheless, certainly in cases of conflicting interests such as on the Sea Islands, developers are well-served to incorporate aspects of this technique into their efforts.

CHAPTER FIVE

The Development of Civil Society

Modern-day nation builders describe civil society as occupying "the political space between the individual and the government." It includes a variety of organizations and activities, all of which "contribute to a democratic society and nonviolent political transition from war to peace" by performing a multitude of functions. Civil society enables citizens to have an impact on government decisions without necessarily competing for political power or resorting to violence. It gives a voice to minority and other marginalized groups. It helps increase government transparency, accountability, and responsiveness.[1]

Developers have increasingly high expectations of civil society. In 1998, United Nations secretary general Kofi Annan heralded it as "the new superpower," claiming "a strong civil society promotes responsible citizenship and makes democratic forms of government work. A weak civil society supports authoritarian rule, which keeps society weak."[2] For many individuals and organizations associated with the Port Royal Experiment, civil society was built upon "the four corner-stones of the church, the school-house, the militia, and the town-meeting," because it was these institutions that provided for "the essential rights of religion, education, self-defense, and self-government."[3] In these areas, civil society made unprecedented, albeit imperfect, progress on the Sea Islands.

The Church and Religion

James Dobbins notes that "in many postconflict societies, civil society organizations are at work prior to the war. When present, the international community should utilize already existing capacity and build on that foundation."[4] Such was the case at Port Royal, where Willie Lee Rose noted that "one form of leadership known to Negroes even in slavery had been the church."[5] Likewise, Edward Pierce, on his initial fact-finding visit in January 1862, found "natural chiefs" had emerged among the black population, in part "by virtue of religious leadership," and he felt these individuals, if "first addressed, may exert a healthful influence on the rest."[6] He also observed the regular and self-regulated church activity of the Sea Islanders.[7] He later wrote, "religion contributes a large part of life's interest to the inhabitants of Port Royal," and it was in this pursuit that he believed that "not only their soul, but their mind finds here its principal exercise."[8] Given this dominant position and head start, the Sea Islanders were quick to enlarge this aspect of civil society. By July 1865, Pierce noted, "nearly the whole church management is now in the hands of the blacks, who have regular deacons and preachers."[9] This ascension of indigenous leadership, however, did not mean the outside developers viewed the church solely as a sterile instrument of civil society. From the start, Pierce's call was for "missionaries," and there would always be an evangelical and denominational component to this aspect of the Port Royal Experiment.[10]

The predominant denomination among the Sea Islanders was Closed-Communion Baptists. This group's practice of restricting participation in the Lord's Supper to church members is one of several ways the freedmen held church membership "in great repute." Membership was granted only after a lengthy period of self-examination, a probationary period in a local subsidiary assembly of "raw souls" called a "society," and baptism. Belonging to a church was considered "a necessary passport to heaven," and "therefore a real power in society."[11]

Church membership was part of the social hierarchy and a means of maintaining order on the Sea Islands. Members were held in high regard and consequently expected to adhere to a higher standard of behavior.[12] Of particular note were the "spiritual mothers and fathers" who were recipients of a special reverence that Laura Towne described as "the most absolute power over" those they had led to baptism.[13] Church membership was

also a way of defining identity, and the practice of closed communion excluded Unitarians such as Towne from participating.
Towne was philosophical about the policy, but upon learning of
it had to "wonder whether it was by [the church's] own wish, or
by instruction that they so decided."[14] Indeed, Towne and others
note several instances of missionaries meddling, often for their
own selfish purposes, in local church affairs.[15]

Clearly, the importance of religion on the Sea Islands and the
emphasis on church membership and denominational affiliation resulted in some friction between the freedmen and the
Gideonites, and even among the Gideonites themselves. Towne,
who otherwise enjoyed friendly relations with a "certain black or
brown [minister] who is certain to make his mark on the world,"
reported the man experienced "intense horror" and said "he
expected better things of me" when he learned she was a Unitarian. The unflappable Towne took the rebuke in stride, noting
the man "is really wonderfully liberal, and, as he will probably
fall in with the right kind of people by reason of his eloquence
and genius, he will one day perhaps be a Unitarian himself."[16]
On a broader front, however, disunity prevailed and grew. Towne
reported a strong wish among the freedmen that "all the white
people would go to the white church and worship together and
leave the black alone in their own brick church."[17] In March 1867,
she opined that the whites were "getting too uppish . . . to associate with blacks, even in church, [and] have determined to have
a white church of their own."[18] She declared "this whole church
plan a snobbish affair, and that there will probably be more rigid
exclusion of blacks from all equality and civility than in the most
snobbish of Northern or Southern churches."[19]

Although Pierce had originally envisioned the freedmen to be
"taught by a pure and plain-spoken Christianity," Gideonites of
various denominations ultimately quarreled among themselves.[20]
Towne found herself displaced from the Brick Church where she
had previously held her classes because the elders there wanted
"to prevent such a large school as ours from being in the hands
of such non-upholders of the Baptist church."[21] Indeed, there was
a steady friction between the evangelical and Unitarian Gideonites.[22] One Northern minister lamented that "he thought he should

The Brick Church, St. Helena Island. Courtesy Library of Congress Prints and Photographs Division Washington, DC.

find peace and zeal down here—a band of fellow workers living in harmony and working with combined effort, but that he finds, friction, friction in every quarter," including the religious one.[23]

In many ways, the rhythm of Sea Islands life revolved around the church. Praise meetings were held three times a week in addition to three more meetings on Sundays.[24] The church also served as a venue for secular activity, collecting money for a memorial to Colonel Robert Shaw, slain commander of the Fifty-Fourth Massachusetts Regiment, and potatoes to be distributed to the soldiers on Morris Island.[25] Churches provided convenient gathering places for meetings such as the one held in the Brick Church on January 17, 1864, to discuss the land issue.[26]

In spite of these positive impacts, religion on the Sea Islands also had proved be a disruptive force that created a factionalism which "nearly reached the dimensions of a gale."[27] By its very nature, religion is a double-edged sword of unity and conflict. A broadly defined Christianity united the freedmen and the Gideonites, both among themselves and each other. From this preexisting condition, a civil society developed around the church. As this process matured, however, conflict also increasingly appeared. Noting that not all civil society is "good," Roland Paris cautions against organizations that "reinforce existing social cleavages, exacerbate tensions, and discourage cross-communal compromise."[28] Likewise, James Dobbins argues that civil society should be both strong and diverse.[29] The church on the Sea Islands certainly met Dobbins's first criteria, but fell short of his second.

The Schoolhouse and Education

Almost inseparably linked to religion during the Port Royal Experiment was education, but this aspect of civil society was buffeted from much of the conflict that sometimes hamstrung church efforts. The Gideonites may have quarreled over many things, but "they were as one on the question of education; this gift seemingly came with no strings attached."[30] As for the Sea Islanders, their appetite for learning was insatiable. One told William Gannett, "We pant for it, sir."[31] Another told Elizabeth Botume, "Us wants to larn, fur we've been in darkness too long, an' now we're in the light, us wants to larn."[32] Superintendents found that "the Negroes . . . will do anything for us, if we only teach them."[33] It was perhaps this mutual enthusiasm and shared purpose that made education "the most successful branch of the experiment."[34]

The Gideonites' brand of education reflected their own experience and their unwavering confidence in the virtues and efficacy of the northern way of life and its methods.[35] "To make another Massachusetts of South Carolina," declared James Thompson, "it is only necessary to give her freedom and education."[36] In providing this education, Edward Atkinson argued, "The tutelary goddess of American liberty should be the pure marble image of the Professor's Yankee school-mistress."[37] As such, the education was part "of a larger socialization process, the objective of which was the mainstreaming of a minority culture into the majority culture."[38] The teachers assumed their own cultural superiority and were often patronizing or condescending to a generally subservient student population.[39] As a result, "their goals were perhaps more moralistic and homiletic than purely social or educational."[40]

Although Pierce's plan called for the provision of "some teachers specially devoted to teaching reading, writing and arithmetic," it was understood that there would be a broad interpretation of the nature and role of education.[41] The appeal for support made to the Boston Educational Commission was clear that although "these agents are called teachers ... their teaching will by no means be confined to intellectual instruction. It will include all the more important and fundamental lessons of civilization,— voluntary industry, self-reliance, frugality, forethought, honesty and truthfulness, cleanliness and order."[42] In this regard, the teachers would become standard-bearers for both Christianity and the free-labor ideology.[43] According to Pierce, the goal of the effort at Port Royal would be to produce "a happy, industrious, law-abiding, free and Christian people."[44] Following this lead, the Boston Educational Commission declared its aim to be "the industrial, social, intellectual, moral and religious elevation of persons released from Slavery in the course of the War for the Union."[45] Indeed, the teachers fulfilled many duties outside the classroom. Charlotte Forten described Towne as "housekeeper, physician, everything, here. The most indispensable person on the place, and the people are devoted to her."[46] Likewise, Edward Everett Hale charged two Boston teachers "to teach [the Sea Islanders] everything which is proper for free men to know," a gamut which Rose notes "included a great deal beyond the ABCs."[47]

In contrast to the case of the church, there was little in the way of established education awaiting the arrival of the Gideonites. In fact, a long history of legal sanctions had prohibited educating blacks for fear of empowering rebellion.[48] Towne did note the exception of Will Capers, a black cabinet maker, who had conducted secret night classes for male slaves.[49] By and large, however, education was a novelty, and the Sea Islanders flocked to the classroom. By the end of 1862, an estimated 1,177 children were in school on St. Helena and Ladies Islands and another 550 at Port Royal.[50] Sometimes entire families came, with mothers bringing children and infants. Botume deftly met this circumstance by arranging for older women to provide care for the infants.[51] More often, the adults came to evening schools, partly to accommodate their work schedules but also to avoid being embarrassed by the children's superior skills.[52] John Rachal declares this effort to reach adults the "first federal role in adult basic education."[53] Although adult formal attendance in school lagged, Pierce reports the salubrious effect of the fact that "nearly every school-child is a teacher in the family."[54] The entire Sea Islands population thus benefited from the multiplicative impact of education.

Dobbins advises, "The international community should help create capacity within civil society organizations that allows them to function according to the rules and procedures set by their boards. Only well-structured organizations can survive 'abandonment' once international organizations leave."[55] The Gideonites attempted to fulfill this charge by establishing school committees patterned after their familiar New England model. Black elders like "Uncle Robert" Chaplin served as chairmen. While the committee members were earnest and passionate about education, they were also largely illiterate.[56] "Only time would tell whether or not such a unique grafting as a New England School Committee could flourish on the stubborn palmetto; the cultural roots of the South Carolina Negro went far back in time, and theirs was indeed a latitude different from that of Boston," Rose mused.[57] As she no doubt suspected, the committees proved ill-equipped to function without the Gideonites.

In fact, the biggest shortcoming in the educational aspect of the Port Royal Experiment was its inability to sustain itself. By 1870, there was a "general exodus" of the teachers who had rushed south in the heady days of the Port Royal Experiment and similar efforts elsewhere.[58] By then, the indefatigable Towne was one of the few remaining stalwarts, and even she lamented, "Our school exists on charity, and charity that is weary."[59] The problem of sustainment is by no means unique to this instance. Dobbins notes that "many international NGOs entering postwar countries fail to create strong local capacity because they largely employ foreign personnel." Instead he argues, "The goal should be to foster and leave behind strong local organizations once they depart."[60] The Avery Normal Institute in Charleston and Towne's own Penn School supplied many teachers to the low country after the departure of the Gideonites, but certainly not enough to fill the need.[61] The result, according to Malcolm Knowles, was "the big tragedy . . . that following the Emancipation Proclamation and the ending of the Civil War adult education was not used as an instrument of national policy to equip the freed slaves to enter the main current of American life on a massive scale."[62]

In recent times, developers have come to consider education to be a basic element of "human security."[63] Indeed, the Universal Declaration of Human Rights pronounces "everyone has the right to education."[64] The Gideonites shared this appreciation of education. Atkinson described it as "the fundamental support of our system," adding "it was education which made us free, progressive, and conservative; and it is education alone which can keep us so."[65] The power of education was accepted as gospel, with many Gideonites considering it as a panacea for all the challenges facing the freedmen.[66] This belief in the change that could be wrought by education, however, was somewhat naïve. Even an advocate like Pierce confided in 1865 that "many friends of the Port Royal movement have a very exaggerated notion of the extent of the education already accomplished there."[67]

Perhaps for this reason, many Gideonites were too quick to declare victory. The Pennsylvania-based Port Royal Relief Commission sent several teachers early on, "but their work was never pushed."[68] Instead, in November 1863, the group declared the work of the relief societies on the Sea Islands "in all aspects an absolute success" and decided to focus its efforts elsewhere.[69] The exception was Towne, whom Pierce proclaimed "the best illustration of permanence and perseverance" he had ever known.[70] In 1871, she vowed "never to leave this 'heathen country'" and declared her intention "to end my days here."[71] She did so, remaining at the helm of her beloved Penn School until her death in 1901. After that, pursuant to arrangements she had made a year before, the school became an auxiliary of the Hampton Institute and was soon renamed the Penn Normal and Industrial School.[72]

By her indefatigable will, Towne had created on St. Helena "an island community virtually isolated from mainland oppressions."[73] But however noble Towne's individual effort, to be effective civil society must be the rule rather than the exception. Dobbins cautions, "While civil society can make an important contribution to the emergence of effective representative government, it cannot offer an alternative. Donors should be wary of using NGOs to deliver services that ought to be provided by the state. Working through such organizations may improve both the quality of the services delivered and accountability for the use of donor funds, but it will do nothing to enhance the capacity of the local government."[74]

This danger is exactly what happened with the Penn School. Towne had sincere and warranted concerns for not allowing her school to be "turned over to the state." "No Northern colored person has a chance of being appointed teacher of a state school," she feared, and she doubted the ability of the school trustees to appoint teachers based on qualification.[75] Besides, as superintendent of schools, she was well aware of the insufficient and sporadic funding and other problems that plagued state schools.[76] Rather than subject her school to such conditions, she jealously guarded her independence, enduring its own challenges to deliver the best possible educational experience to her students. Under the circumstances, it is hard to fault Towne for her approach, and the difference she made in the individual lives of her students is almost indescribable. In spite of this accomplishment, Elizabeth Jacoway concludes, "The Penn School influence touched only a small proportion of the total population, and the great majority of the island blacks remained beyond the reach of [Towne and her assistant Ellen Murray]."[77] Based on this assessment, developers are well-advised to consider the Penn School experience a cautionary tale of the dangers of not building sustainable local capacity.

The Militia and Self-Defense

By the time Major General David Hunter succeeded Major General Thomas Sherman as commander of the Department of the South, the combined forces of the Federal Army and Navy had occupied the strip of coastal islands from about twenty miles south of Charleston to the vicinity of Savannah as well as some isolated coastal points in Georgia and northeast Florida. The Union had long held Key West and soon after Hunter's arrival also had taken Apalachicola and then Pensacola on the Florida Panhandle. Never having more than eighteen thousand troops under his control, Hunter probably had the distinction of commanding the most thinly dispersed body of troops over the largest geographic area in the war. Under such circumstances, Hunter could take little offensive action.[78]

Hunter saw a solution to his personnel problem as well as an outlet for his abolitionist sentiment in the thousands of now masterless slaves within his department. These men represented "a reservoir of loyal manpower that would need only arms and training to augment his army were he able to draw upon it," and Hunter took immediate steps to avail himself of this resource.[79] On April 3, just four days after his arrival, Hunter asked Secretary of War Edwin Stanton for fifty thousand muskets "with authority to arm such loyal men as I can find in the country, whenever, in my opinion, they can be used advantageously against the enemy."[80] Without waiting for Stanton's reply, Hunter enlisted the help of Abram Murchison, an energetic black preacher, to arrange a meeting on Hilton Head to collect the names of blacks willing to "take up arms in defense of the Government and of themselves." The meeting was held on April 7, and Hunter soon had a list of 150 potential volunteers.[81]

By this point, it was obvious that Hunter intended to push the limits of, if not exceed, his authority. He based his actions on instructions originally issued to his predecessor, Sherman, to use blacks as "ordinary employees, or, if special circumstances seem to require it, in any other capacity, with such organization (in squads, companies, or otherwise) as you may deem most beneficial to the service." An important caveat to this authority that Hunter choose to ignore was the specification that "this, however, not being a general arming of them for military service." The official War Department interpretation of these instructions was that blacks could be armed "in cases of great emergency" but "not under regular enrollment for military purposes."[82]

Undeterred from his lack of official endorsement or the fact that, after the initial 150 names, volunteerism among the blacks had stagnated, Hunter on May 8 decided "to enlist two regiments to be officered from the most intelligent and energetic of our non-commissioned officers" and the next day issued an order for his local subordinate commanders "to send immediately to these headquarters, under a guard, all the able-bodied negroes capable of bearing arms."[83] Also on May 9, Hunter took an even bolder step beyond his authority, declaring the emancipation of all slaves in South Carolina, Georgia, and Florida, whether or not within Union lines. Such a measure was not without some precedent, having begun with Major General Ben Butler's pioneering interpretation of the contraband policy at Fort Monroe, Virginia, in May 1861. Then, in August, Major General John Fremont had instituted martial law in Missouri and pronounced the property of all people resisting the United States to be confiscated and their "slaves . . . declared freemen." Even Hunter already had issued an order on April 13, 1862, that the slaves at Fort Pulaski, Georgia, and Cockspur Island were free. Nonetheless, President Abraham Lincoln, taking a pragmatic approach to the war effort writ large, considered such local measures as being premature. He had already voided Fremont's decree, and on May 19, the President also made it clear that Hunter had overstepped his authority.[84]

Hunter's enlistment effort also met resistance from the freedmen. Reluctance to fight their former masters as well as suspicions that the entire proceeding was a ruse to ship them to Cuba "and sell them there," many blacks took "to the woods at the sight of epaulets, guessing their errand."[85] Real volunteers were few, and the conscripts were collected in a manner that certainly did not encourage volunteerism, leading superintendent L. D. Phillips to conclude, "Never, in my judgment, did [a] major-general fall into a sadder blunder and rarely has humanity been outraged by an act of more unfeeling barbarity."[86] According to Pierce, "The men were taken by [Hunter's] soldiers from the field, leaving the hoe standing in the unfinished row, hurried down to Hilton Head, and detained there for three months, subjected to the hostility and insults of all the white regiments."[87] For Towne, the proceedings were too much like the old slave days. "No one likes to be seized and taken from home to unknown parts," she wrote, "especially as they were taught to expect it from their masters."[88]

The strong-armed tactics alienated many potential black soldiers, and Hunter soon abandoned his original plan for two regiments. Even the one regiment he managed to fill was under-strength with as few as eight hundred members.[89] Without much support from Washington, where President Lincoln remained "averse to arming negroes" and with local resistance from both the plantation superintendents and the blacks, an "exasperated" Hunter decided on August 9, 1862, to disband the regiment "for a time" and release the men to "gather crop."[90]

Although Hunter's initial effort had failed, necessity ensured the cause was not to be abandoned. The paucity of Federal soldiers in the Department of the South left the Sea Islands vulnerable to Confederate raids, a fact made abundantly clear to Brigadier General Rufus Saxton as he made a ten-day inspection tour of the coast. Although weapons had been available for some time, Hunter had been reluctant to issue them to the plantations to provide for their defense. That situation changed when Saxton returned from his inspection and learned that the black regiment had been disbanded. On August 16 he wrote a letter to Stanton requesting authority "to enroll as laborers ... a force not exceeding 5,000 able-bodied men from among the contrabands ... to be uniformed, armed, and officered by men detailed from the Army." Avoiding controversy by calling the force "laborers" rather than "soldiers," Saxton's careful wording adroitly negotiated existing policies. Stanton concurred with the proposal and on August 25 authorized Saxton to enroll as many as five thousand black laborers in his service. Then, going beyond Saxton's request, Stanton added,

> In view of the small force under your command and the inability of the Government at the present time to increase it, in order to guard the plantations and settlements occupied by the United States from invasion and protect the inhabitants thereof from captivity and murder by the enemy, you are also authorized to

arm, uniform, equip, and receive into the service of the United
States such number of volunteers of African descent as you may
deem expedient, not exceeding 5,000, and may detail officers to
instruct them in military drill, discipline, and duty, and to command them.[91]

Stanton's letter represented the first official authorization of black
soldiers in the Federal Army.[92] Scholars such as Howard Westwood and Dudley Cornish attribute this outcome to Saxton's deft
handling of the situation, noting the contrast between his diplomatic and well-crafted request and Hunter's ill-conceived and
unilateral assumption of authority.[93]

Even before he began recruiting soldiers, Saxton had twenty
to thirty guns distributed to each plantation for defensive purposes, but efforts to train the blacks on the use of these weapons
met with mixed results.[94] "I have tried in vain to get my young
men together to drill for self-defense," Edward Philbrick complained. The result was his "twenty-five guns are lying useless."
For Philbrick, the reason was clear. "If General Hunter had not
forced them into his regiment last May," Philbrick assessed, "we
might do more drilling now. As it is, my men won't listen to me
when I talk about it; they only suspect me of wanting to press
them into service by stealth, and lose what little confidence they
have in my sincerity."[95]

However frustrated, Philbrick did not give up, and on October
8 reported he had "succeeded day before yesterday in getting thir-
teen of the young men on this plantation to come up and drill,
but they did not come again yesterday."[96] Somehow amid the fits
and starts, the efforts of Philbrick and others came to some effect.
On October 24, 1862, black pickets fired at and repulsed "three
boats full of rebels attempt[ing] to land on these islands."[97] The
threat was not over, and the need for constant vigilance was confirmed on May 21, 1864, when Towne complained Confederates
had raided Morgan Island to the north of St. Helena and "all the
people carried off!" Protests to the local Federal Navy captain,
who claimed "he was put there to blockade and not defend the
coast," were futile.[98] Such an attitude clearly showed the need for
a local defense force.

In the wake of Stanton's authorization to Saxton, when the Emancipation Proclamation went into effect on January 1, 1863, it authorized the freed slaves to "be received into the armed service of the United States" for garrison duty and to man vessels. On January 13, Colonel James Montgomery received authorization from the War Department "to raise, subject to the commanding general of the Department of the South and under his direction, a regiment of South Carolina volunteer infantry, to be recruited in that State, to serve for three years or during the war." On January 25, Saxton reported to Saxton that the organization of the First Regiment of South Carolina Volunteers, commanded by Colonel Thomas Higginson, had been completed and work had begun to fill the Second Regiment to be commanded by Montgomery.[99] Having arrived late of the scene, Montgomery found the "pickings . . . slim," and by March his regiment had just 150 men.[100] One observer mused, "Oh if the formation of the regiment last spring had only been differently managed! we should have a brigade by this time."[101] That opportunity lost, the heavy-handed enlistment measures of 1862 were renewed, and in one incident, Towne reported a dozen armed black soldiers hid in her church, hoping to capture an elusive recruit. To "the great alarm of our children," the soldiers burst forth, but did not find their wanted man among Towne's students. "The colored soldiers ought not to be left to manage this business alone," Towne lamented. "They do not understand yet the proper restrictions of their authority."[102] Others would agree, noting that in spite of "orders not to shoot except in self-defense," soldiers regularly fired at would-be draftees.[103] Such drastic measures were deemed necessary, however, because, as superintendent Charles Ware mused, "for my people, I know there is about as much use in asking them to enlist as in requesting my horse, a very intelligent animal, to drink salt water."[104]

With the advent of more professional recruiting techniques, including the use of bounties, Pierce sensed a complete reversal by the end of the war. By then, he reported, "nearly every able-bodied man is now in uniform; and the letters of those who were most reluctant to go indicate cheerful content and a soldierly pride in the service."[105] In fact, the black regiments were active in the coastal war. Although not locally recruited, the Fifty-Fourth Massachusetts, a regiment of free northern blacks, arrived on the Sea Islands in June 1863 and earned eternal fame for its part in the assault on Fort Wagner in the campaign for Charleston. The Second South Carolina was notorious for what many, including the Fifty-Fourth's commander, Colonel Shaw, considered its barbarous destruction of Darien, Georgia. The "superb" Higginson led the First South Carolina on an expedition into northern Florida and for a time occupied Jacksonville.[106] The military details of these and other operations exceed the scope of this study, but within the context of civil society on the Sea Islands, the contributions of the black regiments were significant. To that end, Massachusetts governor John Andrews need not have worried that blacks would emerge from the Civil War having "lost their masters, but not found a country."[107]

Pierce considered this military training to be unmatched in its importance "to stamp out the past, and to lay a solid foundation for the qualities and habits of their new character,—that of the free Southern laborer."[108] W. Scott Poole notes that the First South Carolina, a regiment made up entirely of former slaves, almost all of whom had come from the Sea Islands and coastal areas, "proved it was possible to triumph even over the soul-destroying effects of chattel slavery."[109] For Rose, it was the experience of military service that "would more than any other fix the status of the Negro as a free man."[110] It would also prove to be useful training for the "black militias" that for a time after the war, in the low country anyway, served as an effective foil against white violence.

The Town Meeting and Self-Government

Of the "four cornerstones of civil society," the most difficult to achieve was the self-government intended to be borne of the town meeting. Political life on the Sea Islands whiplashed from its days as "black paradise" under Radical Reconstruction to "white redemption" with the election of Wade Hampton as governor. Rose explains the reversal by quoting the First South Carolina's Colonel Higginson, who said that "revolutions may go backward."[111] Roland Paris would perhaps ascribe the result to the dangers of not achieving "institutions before liberalization."[112] In spite of the ultimate reversal, the Port Royal Experiment succeeded in establishing the town meeting as a forum of discourse on the Sea Islands.

Drawing on the New England tradition, many of the town meetings held on the Sea Islands were of a political nature. At a meeting in May 1864 that William Gannett deemed as "probably the first time that the slaves—contrabands—freedmen—have asserted themselves our fellow-countrymen by claiming the right of voting," delegates were elected to the National Union Convention to be held in Baltimore, Maryland on June 7.[113] Gannett reported "a large half of the meeting consisted of blacks," and four blacks, including Robert Smalls, were selected.[114] In May, 1867, Towne excitedly wrote the black St. Heleners "are busy forming a Republican Party on the island."[115] At a mass meeting of Republican citizens," she reported the speakers were all black men, except for [John] Hunn, and the debate centered on the future of political cooperation with whites. In the end, it was decided to invite "all colors to another grand mass meeting next Saturday."[116] To Towne's chagrin, however, it was decided that women would not be allowed to attend the meetings. Citing the patriarchal attitude of the male blacks, Towne snipped, "When women get the vote, too, no people will be more indignant than these, I suppose."[117] Reflecting the changing times, by 1876 there were Democrat meetings as well, "miserably small," sniffed Towne, "but large enough for Republican Beaufort."[118]

While political meetings attracted the most attention, they were far from the only examples of this type of civil society. With the war still waging elsewhere, the Sea Islanders gathered to mark the Fourth of July in 1863 by singing such patriotic songs as "The Star Spangled Banner" and reading the Declaration of Independence.[119] Harriet Ware reported being very pleased that Judge Abram Smith, who presided over a public meeting in April 1864 to address a petition filed against Edward Philbrick, "could not have dust thrown in his eyes" by the "palpably absurd" allegations.[120] In April 1869, Sea Islanders gathered to determine a collective strategy to confront white efforts to recover land.

Reflecting a philosophy of strength in numbers, Towne reported the decision to "get first-rate counsel and pay for it by combined effort."[121] As time passed, the range of topics expanded. In February 1870, Towne boasted of a temperance society called the "St. Helena Band of Hope," which held "regular meetings every fortnight."[122] Children were taught temperance songs and performed topical skits. According to Towne, they "enjoy it highly, and even the littlest want to join." Organization and procedures had also advanced, with Towne noting attendees were expected to "follow 'Parliamentary rules.'"[123] In June 1877, she described a large district school meeting "of the most influential men among the blacks of the island," with Towne and a man "representing the whites." The meeting voted to pay a tax in support of the public schools. By this time, Towne reported the result of such civil society was "our little island has been expressing itself" and "the St. Helena folks are awake to their rights."[124]

The fleeting nature of these rights quickly became apparent with the end of Reconstruction and the election of Democrat Wade Hampton as governor in 1877. First armed and organized groups of whites called Red Shirts and then a series of laws reminiscent of the Black Codes made it more and more difficult for blacks to assemble for political or other purposes. Still, with Beaufort County's thirty thousand blacks comprising 80 percent of the population, Robert Smalls was able to continue his political leadership for another twenty years from what became known as the "Black District."[125] However, this self-government that Rose describes as "the last turning of the wheel of the revolution" proved to be only a temporary reality for the Sea Island blacks, ultimately succumbing to the growing tide of statewide white supremacy.[126]

The Struggle for Civil Society

Donald Mitchell contends that "public space is a space of conflict, of political tussle, of social relations stripped to their barest essentials."[127] If civil society is "the political space between the individual and the government," it cannot expect to be immune from this struggle.[128] Indeed, all four aspects of civil society on the Sea Islands were scenes of active competition.

The church suffered from denominational strife, both among the Gideonites and between the Gideonites and the freedmen. Eventually, the churches on the Sea Islands went the way of most churches in America and divided themselves along not just denominational but racial lines as well. The schoolhouse experienced a struggle for control, and Towne ultimately opted for autonomy rather than the vagaries of the state system. In the process, she may have achieved tactical victory but strategic defeat. Like the rest of the Jim Crow South, public education on the Sea Islands devolved into unequal institutions for blacks and whites. Given the state of war, the militia was by nature a scene of conflict, but even after the peace, black and white militias continued the violence. The town meeting is designed as a forum for debate, so productive conflict within its space is expected and welcomed. However, the competition for political control of the Sea Islands soon became an all-or-nothing brawl between Republicans and Democrats divided predominantly along racial lines.

In hindsight it appears that the dizzying growth of civil society wrought by the Port Royal Experiment was largely "a mile wide and an inch deep." Rather than self-sustaining, institutionalized changes, it was artificially propped up by the presence of the Gideonites, Freedmen's Bureau, U.S. Army, and other outside actors. When these influences withdrew, the competition for the space occupied by civil society resumed under terms decisively advantageous to whites committed to controlling society. Whatever its temporary accomplishments, the Port Royal Experiment failed Dobbins's requirement to establish "a civil society that can exist without external support over time."[129]

CHAPTER SIX

Refugees and Families

Violence in today's world is marked less by interstate conflict and more by internal strife and civil war than it has been in the past. Therefore, although the words are often used almost interchangeably, there are now fewer refugees and more internally displaced persons (IDPs). Nonetheless, these IDPs are often exposed to the same difficult situations common to refugees who flee to neighboring countries.[1] The Port Royal Experiment was beset both by IDPs created by the sudden collapse of the slaveocracy and refugees, many of whom came to the Sea Islands in the wake of Major General William Sherman's March through Georgia. If we treat IDPs and refugees as a collective group, the Sea Islands experience offers valuable insights into the enduring humanitarian problem which Poul Hartling, former United Nations High Commissioner for Refugees, has described as being "the massive arrivals of refugees in low-income countries where often no durable solutions are at hand."[2] These three conditions—massive arrivals, low-income, and no durable solutions—provide a convenient format for analyzing the IDP and refugee situation on the Sea Islands.

Massive Arrivals

"Massive" is relative term, and the ability of a society to absorb refugees is largely a function both of the number of the refugees and their rate of arrival. The Sea Islands were besieged by total numbers that saturated the available infrastructure at a rate that exceeded the throughput capacity. At its peak, the overall population of Sea Islands blacks had increased by over 50 percent, and on some single days, refugees amounting to nearly 9 percent of the prewar population arrived in the area. Such quantities simply overwhelmed available resources.

In his initial survey, dated February 3, 1862, Edward Pierce estimated a population of some eight thousand blacks under Federal protection on Sea Island plantations. Already, however, additions such as "negroes who have fled to Beaufort and Hilton Head from places not yet occupied by our forces" had swelled to nearly twelve thousand the number "we must now have thrown upon our hands, for whose present and future we must provide."[3] Elizabeth Hyde Botume wrote that Beaufort was "overflowing," and people "were quartered in every available place, and packed as closely as possible,—in churches and storehouses, and in the jail and arsenals." Nonetheless, Botume lamented that "there was still a great throng houseless, with no resting-place."[4] The worst was yet to come, with Pierce noting the number of new arrivals was "rapidly increasing."[5]

In addition to outside refugees, internally displaced persons also added to the instability. An early instance occurred in July 1862, when Major General David Hunter ordered the withdrawal of Federal troops from Edisto Island in order to concentrate his defenses. "Edisto is evacuated!," Laura Towne exclaimed, "and all the negroes brought to these islands." Beaufort was already "overcrowded with refugees," and the 1,600 new arrivals from Edisto, "with their household effects, pigs, chickens, and babies 'promiscuous,'" were sent to St. Helenaville, once a health resort that boasted a dozen or more mansions.[6] Another category of people arrived as Colonels James Montgomery and Thomas Higginson launched coastal raids to liberate slaves from Confederate rice plantations. One of the more notable of these expeditions was the June 1863 raid on Combahee that brought to Beaufort eight hundred members of "as poor and destitute a class of human beings as could possibly be found."[7] As a result of all these sources, a steady stream of homeless blacks needing most all manner of care and services soon found themselves in the midst of the Port Royal Experiment.

The problem dramatically worsened as Major General William Sherman marched across Georgia from Atlanta to Savannah in late 1864. In his wake, countless slaves fled to his lines while others dispersed into the countryside. Reports vary as to how many refugees actually arrived at the coast with the Sherman, but Major General Henry Slocum, who commanded the left wing of Sherman's march, estimated that seven thousand were still with the army when it reached Savannah.[8] Along the way, the wayfarers had endured much hardship, and for these suffering, homeless masses, the beckoning of the Sea Islands was "as clear as the polar star."[9] Even as Sherman presented Savannah "as a Christmas gift" to President Abraham Lincoln, "seven hundred cold, shivering, and hungry freedmen ... in the direst need of every human requirement" were arriving at Beaufort.[10] Others soon followed in similar straits. Towne reported "very many come sick: indeed, nearly all are broken down with fatigue, privation of food, and bad air at night."[11] Botume wrote that "with the army came a great gang of contrabands to be housed and rationed and taken care of."[12]

The numbers were staggering. Even with today's improved technological capabilities, getting accurate refugee counts is problematic, and contemporary reports from the Port Royal Experiment were further complicated by inconsistencies in geographic area of the count. In broad terms, however, Willie Lee Rose estimates "the Negro population ... swelled from less than ten thousand at the time of the Federal occupation to more than fifteen thousand, even before any Sherman refugees arrived."[13] After this growth of over 50 percent, how many of the perhaps seven thousand blacks who arrived in Savannah with Sherman then migrated north to the immediate area around Port Royal and how long they stayed are unknown. Some idea of the magnitude can be extrapolated from census data showing an increase in the black population of St. Helena Parish from 7,673 in 1860 to 11,063 in 1870, a 44 percent growth that Hermine Baumhofer attributes in part to blacks "from other parts of South Carolina, who drifted to the Sea Islands during the war in order to gain their freedom and the chance to own land."[14] In more recent memory, an influx of refugees from Kosovo into neighboring Macedonia in 1999 represented less than a 20 percent population increase yet threatened to destabilize the fledgling country and attracted a massive international response to avert a humanitarian catastrophe.[15] Proportionately, the refugee situation with which the Port Royal Experiment had to cope exceeded this scope and certainly can be characterized as massive.

Low-Income Environment

The size of the refugee problem on the Sea Islands was exacerbated by the area's dearth of what modern advocates consider to be basic "human security." This understanding of society emphasizes the importance of the basic necessities, quality of life, and individual dignity humans need to feel secure. War and large displacements of populations threaten this sense of human security, especially in areas already operating on the margins.[16] On the Sea Islands, existing housing was substandard; food, clothing, medical care, and other essentials were in short supply; and provisions for women, children, and families were severely strained. The result was a low-income environment struggling to sustain itself, let alone accommodate a massive influx of refugees.

In his initial survey, Pierce described the slave quarters as each being assigned to a family and measuring sixteen feet by twelve feet. They were generally open, although some interiors were divided into sections by a partition. While conditions varied, Pierce found between ten and twenty sets of slave quarters on the plantations he visited.[17] Many were in poor repair, such as the "wretched hovels" Towne found at the old Jenkins, Fripp, and Edding's Point properties.[18] Austere to begin with, these houses certainly offered little hope of accommodating large numbers of refugees. The abandoned planters' homes provided relief for a fortunate few, but certainly not enough to make more than a small dent in the overall demand.[19] Even among these, Charles Ware considered the "big house" at the McTureous plantation to be "old, rickety, poorly put together and shabbily kept."[20] Moreover, in the exuberance that accompanied the flight of their

Port Royal slave quarters as they appeared in 1862. Courtesy Library of Congress Prints and Photographs Division Washington, DC.

masters, many of the slaves had destroyed wantonly furniture, beds, and other household items for which there was now a great need.[21] The shortage of available housing and shelter complicated the Sea Islands' ability to accommodate refugees, and with all existing housing in use, tents were used as a stopgap measure until barracks were built.[22]

Typical of the newly constructed housing was the village built to accommodate the refugees from Montgomery's raids. Botume described these houses as resembling "huge wooden boxes" divided into four rooms. Each room was equipped with a fireplace, an opening for a window with a shutter, a double row of "berths" built against the wall for beds, one or more low benches, a pine table, and homemade cedar tubs. Each of these rooms accommodated a family of between five and fifteen members.[23] As in many modern refugee situations, adult women made up a large percentage of the population; in this case because many of the men were now serving in Montgomery's regiment.[24] The women made the best of the situation as they could, and Botume, finding herself "face to face with life in the 'one-roomed cabin,'" was favorably impressed by the fortitude of the occupants of these meager dwellings.[25]

As plain as were these accommodations, their residents were fortunate compared to the refugees who lived in tents until barracks space became available. Botume reported these souls suffered through an "unusually severe" winter "without fire or a floor," and smallpox swept through the camp. Some selfless individuals exchanged their rooms for tents to provide some relief to those afflicted.[26]

The region's preexisting low-income level explains much of this vulnerability. Emerging from slavery, the native Sea Islanders were scarcely able to meet their own survival needs, let alone provide substantial assistance to refugees. After his victory at Port Royal, Flag Officer Samuel Du Pont reported finding a black population "almost starving and some naked or nearly so."[27] Pierce reported the slaves subsisted on a deficient diet that was "mainly vegetable."[28] As bad as the situation was for the native population in Beaufort, Botume observed that "the refugees were vastly worse off than the plantation people. They literally had nothing to wear, and the weather had become very cold."[29]

In spite of these dire straits, Botume was impressed, however mixed the results, with the efforts to maintain family unity that she observed.[30] Indeed, a variety of studies identify the correlation between the strength of the family unit and other aspects of development. Research conducted by the United Nations, for example, concludes that "good overall development of the child in poverty is a product of high-quality child care, taking place mainly at the level of the well-functioning family. Children thriving in poor communities were statistically most likely to live in families characterized by traditional fireside family values, devoted mothers and fathers, happy marriages, and warm cooperative bonds with siblings, grandparents, other relatives, and the broader community."[31] Unfortunately, such conditions did not exist on the Sea Islands, where isolation had compounded the serious disruption imposed upon the black family structure by slavery.[32]

The institution of marriage was at best ill-defined in the slave community. Oftentimes without the benefit of clergy, "the marriage ceremony in most cases consisted of the slaves simply getting the master's permission and moving into a cabin together."[33] Traditions such as "jumping the broomstick" served to transform a free union into a marriage, and "marrying in blankets" was accomplished by a woman bringing her bedroll beside that of the man to whom she pledged her love and commitment.[34] Gideonites typically were told, "No, not married, ma'am, I just took her and brought her home" to inquiries about marital status.[35] For Pierce, such nonchalance represented a perception of marriage as being "as much a matter of convenience and necessity as of affection."[36] Thus, he reported it "not uncommon to form a second marriage within a few weeks after death has severed the first."[37] The decision was largely a pragmatic one, and especially among male slaves, love mattered little in entering a marriage. As Robert Smalls explained, "The colored men in taking wives always do so in reference to the service the women will render."[38]

Families ties "were made and severed at the owner's will," and couples who resided on different plantations were only allowed to visit with the consent of their masters.[39] For Pierce, these forced separations represented the "buryings alive of slavery."[40] He also noted that since "the children go with the mother, it is the owner's advantage to have all his men marry on his plantation." This practice, he thought, contributed to intermarriage, adultery, and immorality.[41]

Children fathered either by a fellow slave or by a member of the plantation hierarchy were plentiful, and suitable child care was lacking.[42] Teacher Ellen Murray reported she could "not find a girl over sixteen that was not a mother."[43] Pierce agreed that "the yards seemed to swarm with children" as a result of "the negroes coupling at an early age."[44] Slave mothers returned to the fields three or four weeks after giving birth and then saw the baby during the day only long enough for feeding. Rather than a happy occasion of bonding, Rose describes this duty as "merely an additional drain upon a tired body."[45] In the meantime, small children were superintended by superannuated "Maumas" whom many Gideonites decried as abusive or incompetent.[46] Pierce reported that "we have never seen parents more apathetic," because slavery had conditioned mothers to consider "their children are hardly their own."[47]

This outcome was the result of decades of reinforcement. Since 1808, "the importation of slaves into any port or place within the jurisdiction of the United States ... from any foreign kingdom, place, or country" had been illegal.[48] However, with over four million slaves already in the South, slavery was self-sustaining in that children of slaves automatically became slaves themselves. Thus, Pierce noted that "child-bearing was systematically encouraged by the owner," leading mothers to view their baby only as "one more little nigger for Massa."[49] Likewise, Laura Towne concluded mothers devoted little concern to their babies' welfare, "thinking it 'massa's' concern whether it was kept alive or not."[50] Another result of this reliance on the plantation as provider was "the annihilation by slavery, to the great extent, of the father in the domestic relations of the slaves."[51] Indeed, Towne found that "in slavery, the woman was far more important, and was in every way held higher than the man. It was the woman's house, the children were entirely hers, etc."[52] Setting the causes aside, the Gideonites certainly found little evidence of what they considered to be responsible parenting by either the mother or the father.

Under such circumstances, infant mortality soared, with Pierce reporting some families suffering 50 percent fatalities. Due to "the constant labor" slave mothers were forced to perform, as well as "ignorance and carelessness," Pierce found "a vast number of infants perish before they are three years old."[53] Like Towne, Pierce noted that mothers expressed little sense of loss over the death of a child, explaining that "the rough pressure of slavery tends especially to crush the tender expression of feeling."[54]

Abhorred by what they found, the Gideonites made a concerted effort "to regularize Negro family life, to make it conform to the accepted pattern," including encouraging fathers to assume previously unknown responsibilities.[55] As part of this program, on August 22, 1862, Brigadier General Rufus Saxton issued General Order No. 7, which tasked Mansfield French with sorting through the tangle of relationships to determine which marriages were lawful and to compel men with more than one "wife" to legally marry the one who was the mother of his children and live with her only. Declaring that "the sacred institution of Marriage lies at the very foundation of all civil society," Saxton continued the effort by issuing General Order No. 8 on August 11, 1865, which specified "marriage rules" that outlined the duties of married couples and specified who was eligible to marry and to perform the ceremonies.[56] Pierce was impressed by the results, and in 1865 remarked that "the women, being no longer mere field-laborers, spend much more time in household employments and with their children." Indeed, he considered both mothers and fathers to have become "gentler and more apt to caress the young ones." He noted with pride that "many weddings have been celebrated in church," spouses were faithfully discharging their "reciprocal duties," marital quarrels had been reduced, and "for a separation and second marriage an appeal to the law is necessary." "Family feeling," he concluded, "appears to have gained strength and purity."[57]

Nonetheless, Pierce noted that the effects of four or five generations of slavery would not be erased overnight.[58] The human security and other problems that plagued native and refugee Sea Islanders were persistent and deep. In such a repressed environment, relative improvement could be quickly achieved, but durable solutions would be required to sustain any gains and establish a new elevated standard of living.

No Durable Solutions

Such solutions require a level of commitment across a broad spectrum of efforts. The initial energy, interest, and positive

attitude must be maintained. Programs must address the under-
lying cause of the problem rather than merely the superficial situation, and resources must be sufficient to meet the need. Finally,
political will must be sustained to provide vision and weather
inevitable challenges and setbacks. All these factors add up to the
perseverance that a host of observers has concluded is critical to
successful development.[59]

Among the causes of initial hopefulness in assimilating the
refugees was Pierce's observation that the Sea Islanders' understanding of "family" was a broad one. "Everyone," he noted, "is
aunt or uncle or cousin to everyone else."[60] Given the infrastructure's small capacity to absorb the influx of refugees, it was fortunate that this inclusive approach meant "hospitality, which is ever
ready, [and] may be taxed as a right by all the kin."[61] Nonetheless,
outsiders still faced obstacles to acceptance. Botume observed that
her Beaufort students initially "had been rather unfriendly to the
refugees, always passing them with a degree of scorn, and speak-
ing of them as 'dem rice niggers.'" With the passage of time, however, she reported "now they were entirely ready to fraternize."[62]

A more serious challenge to acceptance was presented when
Sherman's arrival in Savannah initiated a new wave of refugees
that further strained the Sea Islands' already meager resources.
The native St. Heleners were understandably ambivalent about
still more newcomers and were less than welcoming. Edward
Philbrick reported that the more generous hospitality came
from the earlier arrivals from Edisto who still had "their own
recent destitution fresh in mind." "Look 'o we," Philbrick typified
the Edisto outlook. "We come here wi' noffin at all [and] now
we have money for cotton and all the tater and hominy we can
eat." With a mixture of accomplishment and magnanimity, one
women declared, "Bress the Lord, I have striven and got enough
to give seven gowns to these poor folk."[63] Towne also declared
the "open-hearted charity" of this group to be "astonishing."[64] As
impressive as the response was, it was still a temporary solution,
and to relieve the overcrowding, Saxton announced his intention
to reoccupy Edisto "pretty soon."[65]

Saxton had little time to deliberate over this course of
action. After being resupplied in Savannah, Sherman received

This dock at Hilton Head built by Federal troops served as a temporary camp site for refugees. Courtesy Library of Congress Prints and Photographs Division Washington, DC.

authorization to march northward on January 2, 1865.[66] Eager to advance but faced with a massive logistical problem that threatened his mobility, he made the pragmatic decision to issue Special Field Order No. 15 on January 16. Based on immediate military necessity rather than long-term social policy, the order seized as federal property "the islands from Charleston, south, the abandoned rice fields along the rivers for thirty miles back from the sea, and the country bordering the St. Johns River,

Florida." This property would be reserved "for the settlement of the negroes now made free by the acts of war and the proclamation of the President of the United States."[67] As far as a "durable solution" goes, however, Sherman insisted in his *Memoirs* that "all that was designed by these special field orders was to make temporary provisions for the freedmen and their families during the rest of the war, or until Congress should take action in the premises."[68]

Under the order, the hardworking, but by now chagrined, Saxton was made Inspector of Settlements and Plantations, and he quickly began holding mass meetings to explain the procedures to the freedmen. Many of the earlier refugees from Edisto promptly returned home and others from Georgia joined them. In some cases, resettlement proceeded in orderly fashion, as at Skidaway Island, Georgia, but with scores of freedmen descending on Sherman's reserve as the Federal Army passed through the Carolinas, the ability to absorb the swelling numbers quickly was overwhelmed. Temporary camps on the docks at Hilton Head and Savannah lacked necessary shelter and sanitation, and thousands died there.[69] The situation was exacerbated in Beaufort by the presence of Sherman's army, which nearly exhausted the already-limited supplies as it passed through.[70] Recognizing this problem, today's military doctrine cautions that "military forces should not compete for scarce civilian resources" in humanitarian disaster areas.[71]

As the relief agencies struggled to cope, they appealed to the government for help. The result was the creation of Bureau of Refugees, Freedmen, and Abandoned Lands on March 3, 1865. The act that created the Bureau granted the authority "to set apart, for the use of loyal refugees and freedmen, such tracts of land within the insurrectionary states as shall have been abandoned, or to which the United States shall have acquired title by confiscation or sale, or otherwise, and to every male citizen, whether refugee or freedman, as aforesaid, there shall be assigned not more than forty acres of such land." Those individuals assigned the land could rent it at a fixed rate and, at the end of the three-year period or before, could "purchase the land and receive such title thereto as the United States can convey." While some observers viewed this clause as legalizing the claims based on Sherman's earlier order, subsequent events would show that even this act did not represent a durable solution and that much of the land returned to its previous white ownership.[72]

One casualty of this restoration policy was Mitchelville, one of the best examples of a potentially durable solution to the living situation for Sea Island blacks. As early as October 1862, critics had argued that "the present negro quarters—a long row of partitions into which are crowded young and old, male and female, without respect either to quality or quantity, such has thus far been the necessity— . . . [have] become a sort of Five Points [an allusion to a dilapidated section of Manhattan], half style, half brothel."[73] Among those who saw a better alternative was Major General Ormsby Mitchel, a multitalented West Pointer who had been assigned to South Carolina after running afoul of Major General Don Carlos Buell during the Federal Army's occupation of North Alabama. Presaging Major General William Sherman's policy of "hard war," Mitchel found himself at odds with Buell's conciliatory approach to the Confederate population. As a result, Mitchel was recalled to Washington, was briefly sent to the Midwest on recruiting duty, and then was appointed commander of the Department of the South.[74]

In this new capacity, Mitchel selected the Drayton Plantation on Hilton Head as the site of a unique "experiment in citizenship" to develop "an actual town" rather than the earlier camps and barracks. According to Mitchel's plan, which was consistent with free-labor ideology, "the negroes are to be made to build their own houses, and it is thought to be high time they should begin to learn what freedom means by experience of self-dependence, they are to be left as much as possible to themselves."[75] With its neatly arranged streets and quarter-acre lots, Mitchelville certainly looked the part, but beyond these aesthetic improvements also lay a town government with a mayor and treasurer appointed by the military commander and a town supervisor, council, recorder, and marshal elected by the black residents. The mayor and the council comprised a board of administration that maintained a compulsory public school system for children ages six to fifteen, levied and collected taxes, adjudicated minor

Map of Mitchelville, circa 1865. Courtesy National Archives.

disputes, and regulated sanitation and community behavior to include "due observance of the Lord's Day."[76]

Organized communities such as Mitchelville were consistent with what black spokesman Garrison Frazier had expressed during Secretary of War Edwin Stanton's visit to Major General William Sherman's army in January 1865, namely that blacks would "prefer to live by ourselves [rather than interspersed among whites], because there is a prejudice against us in the South that will take years to get over."[77] Indeed, Mitchelville survived into the 1870s as a vibrant community that produced a "sizable 'black yeomanry' class."[78] Succumbing to a variety of pressures, however, in the early 1880s, Mitchelville lost its character as a town and became a small, kinship-based community.[79] Much of this demise can be traced to the federal land restoration policy that resulted in the Drayton Plantation being returned to the heirs of its former owner in April 1875.

Although the federal government deed failed to provide any protection for Mitchelville, the Drayton heirs were not interested in planting the lands and put them up for sale. A successful black man named March Gardner was able to buy most of Mitchelville, which at this time also included a store, cotton gin, and grist mill. Gardner put his son Gabriel in charge of Mitchelville and also trusted Gabriel to have a proper deed made out. Instead, Gabriel took advantage of the situation and eventually obtained a deed in his own name and then transferred the property to his wife and daughter. Rather than a "durable solution," this was the beginning of further chicanery and mismanagement that led to "a sad end to what was the birthplace of freedom for many Sea Island blacks." White investors, including Roy Rainey of New York, increasingly bought tracts of Hilton Head land, and by the late 1930s, only three hundred blacks remained of a population of nearly three thousand in 1890.[80] Such a turn of events certainly represented a marked departure from whatever promise Mitchelville once had for its black residents.

Observations

Refugees remain a continuing threat to an individual's expectation of human security as well as a state's national security, however these are defined. The Gideonites, the Army, and the government were ill-equipped to handle the crisis on the Sea Islands. Today, international government organizations such as the United Nations through its high commissioner for refugees, U.S. government bureaucracies such as the Federal Emergency Management Agency, and nongovernmental organizations like Oxfam and the American Red Cross are much better resourced, equipped, prepared, and experienced in dealing with such crises. Still, success remains elusive. For example, the Congressional Select Bipartisan Committee to Investigate the Preparation for the Response to Hurricane Katrina found that "relocation plans did not adequately provide for shelter. Housing plans were haphazard and inadequate."[81] It is hardly fair to expect something more in 1862.

Family strength and resilience remain important concerns within the context of refugee situations and overall human security. The Gideonites' attempt to improve families on the Sea Islands raises two questions relevant to aid workers, developers, governments, and other actors. The first involves whether or not family issues are a purely personal matter or a legitimate target for policy making. Certainly, the Gideonites thought families were a proper focus, and Karen Bogenschneider argues that modern American political judgments and polling data support this assessment.[82] Efforts to legislate family behavior are controversial, but Bogenschneider notes that one way or another, "most laws, or lack thereof, have some impact on family life."[83] Certainly, Saxton's General Orders No. 7 and 8 represent very direct efforts to create government-directed family policy. Pierce, at least, determined them to have been successful.

The second question is a little more complicated. When passionate Gideonites like Austa French boasted of their efforts "to impose the decencies of family customs in living, eating and worshipping, upon those so debased in habits and utterly irregular," all manner of questions about cultural bias come to the fore.[84] The Gideonites represented what might today be called the "concerned" approach to family matters. This view focuses on negative consequences of changes to the family, such as those the Gideonites attributed to slavery. Their family values include parental commitment, marital fidelity, individual responsibility, and civic participation.[85] Like James Thompson, who sought "to make another Massachusetts of South Carolina," the concerned camp believes that broad cultural change is possible and that they know which direction that change should take.[86] While the Gideonites received little challenge to this set of assumptions, today's family advocates must be much more sensitive to alternative understandings of the family and must pursue a much more balanced approach.[87]

In spite of the Gideonites' recognition of the importance of the family and their assessment of the institution's weakness on the Sea Islands, they do not appear to have developed a focused, deliberate effort to train parents on specific child management techniques such as closer monitoring, conveying clear expectations for behavior, responding effectively to noncompliance, and rewarding positive behavior. Such parental instruction has been proven to be a cost-effective means of strengthening families.[88] Instead, Gideonites understandably focused their educational efforts on children. Few adults attended schools, often considering themselves "too old or too busy" for education.[89] Such self-selection notwithstanding, the Gideonites also "were not wholly prepared" to meet the demands of educating adults, and their efforts were uncoordinated and haphazard.[90]

The refugee crisis on the Sea Islands reinforces Hartling's call for durable solutions. While temporary shelter may be the most visibly urgent need for refugees and IDPs, only well-thought-out policy and sustained commitment can solve problems in the long term. These requirements were absent on the Sea Islands.

The Port Royal Experiment was more successful as a fledgling example of the process of needs assessment that looks beyond the obvious requirement for shelter to determine other refugee needs in the broad category of human security. The Gideonites identified strengthening the family as one such need and, to their great credit, devoted considerable energy in this area. Their effectiveness was limited by some factors beyond their control, such as inadequate resources, as well as their own dubious qualifications for such an undertaking. Advances in the academic discipline of child and family studies have better equipped their successors for such a role, and the family as a matter of public policy is now much better understood. Nonetheless, today's family professionals remain "underfinanced, poorly staffed, loosely organized, and overcommitted"—just like the Gideonites were.[91]

CHAPTER SEVEN

Economic Development and Land Redistribution

The Port Royal Experiment pursued economic development in terms of the three fronts Edward Pierce, in his initial report to Secretary of the Treasury Salmon Chase, identified as "what could be done to reorganize the laborers, prepare them to become sober and self-supporting citizens, and secure the successful culture of a cotton-crop."[1] Integral to Pierce's objective to "reorganize the laborers" was the issue of land distribution. Efforts to produce "sober and self-supporting citizens" would proceed in accordance with the free-labor ideology. Finally, the prized Sea Island cotton, either as a source of revenue for a cash-strapped Lincoln administration, as a means of funding the development effort, or as a source of personal profit, lay at the center of all economic decisions. Thus, economic development on the Sea Islands involved the timeless considerations of control of the area's principal natural resource, the individual and his pursuit of happiness, and a state directed land policy.

Cotton

It did not take the Lincoln administration long to recognize the economic value of Sea Island cotton, and it was always a consideration in selecting Port Royal as the target for Flag Officer Samuel Du Pont's attack. Writing on September 30, 1861, Attorney General Edward Bates said, "I do trust that the naval expedition to the southern coast, will not be delayed much longer."

The attorney general added that he was "credibly informed . . . from 3 to 4 million dollars' worth of Sea Island cotton, now in the course of harvest . . . is easily within our reach." To Bates, this bounty represented "merchandize [sic], ready to our hand."[2] With the same understanding, Pierce, in his February 3, 1862, report to Secretary Chase, provided thorough details of the agricultural cycle, emphasizing that the cotton crop "for this season was unusually good."[3] While the military value of Port Royal as a base from which to support the blockade was the key strategic consideration, the economic possibilities presented by Sea Island cotton certainly would not be ignored.

James Dobbins notes that natural resources represent a potential source of conflict, and the intervening authorities need to make securing them a high priority.[4] To this end, Secretary Chase dispatched Lieutenant Colonel William Reynolds who, by December 20, 1861, was in Beaufort as the U.S. agent to collect contraband cotton.[5] Soon, Attorney General Bates gleefully reported that "cotton in great quantities . . . is being gathered by the army as fast as possible, to be sen[t] north."[6] Fortunately, proceeds from this "Contraband Fund" offset the fact that the government lost between fifty and seventy-five thousand dollars the first planting season. Beset by a variety of problems, only 3,384 acres had been planted on the principal islands of Hilton Head, Port Royal, and St. Helena, yielding 90,000 pounds of ginned product according to the highest estimate. The result was a disappointing yield of lint cotton of less than twenty-six pounds per acre. Before the war, St. Helena had produced annual average yields as high as 130 pounds per acre, and one Edisto Island plantation had sustained an average yield of 137 pounds per acre over the previous eighteen years.[7] Even after chronicling the difficulties and trying to portray the "noble cause" in the best possible light, Pierce had to confess that "as a whole, the crop of 1862 was not sufficient to cover the year's expenses."[8] Having applied the hard lessons learned, Pierce points to improvement in the crop of 1863. Without citing any figures, he surmises that year's crop "probably paid, besides its own expenses, the deficit in the previous year's income."[9]

As far as the development effort was concerned, however, there was more to the issue than mere generation of income. Also of importance was where that income went. Martin Abbott, citing an 1865 report by Brigadier General Rufus Saxton, estimates some three hundred thousand dollars in proceeds was created by the sale of Sea Island cotton, but this income went to Secretary Chase's Treasury Department instead of the Freedmen's Bureau, the agency tasked with aiding the indigenous population. Likewise, whatever income the Bureau hoped to generate from the sale and rental of abandoned and confiscated land, including some three hundred thousand acres on the Sea Islands, evaporated with President Andrew Johnson's order of September 1865 that resulted in the return of the bulk of the land to its former owners. As a result of this policy, by 1866, the Bureau's rental income had dropped to fifty dollars a month from the six thousand dollars a month it had collected a year earlier. The significance of these developments is that in creating the Freedmen's Bureau, Congress allocated no funds for it, instead believing the Bureau could generate its own income. Without the anticipated proceeds from cotton and land, Abbott notes, "the inevitable result was a sharp curtailment in [the Bureau's] program at a time when the need for its assistance among the people was greatest."[10]

This idea of developing natural resources to pay for a nation building operation continues to be as attractive as it is elusive. On March 27, 2003, Deputy Defense Secretary Paul Wolfowitz promised the House Appropriations Committee that in Iraq, "We're dealing with a country that can really finance its own reconstruction, and relatively soon."[11] Instead, critics claimed the U.S. presence in Iraq became a "cash-cow" for private contractors.[12] Likewise in Afghanistan, one observer reported, "who knows anymore—what is an NGO and what is a company, given the salaries today."[13] In similar fashion, William Gannett noted that as events unfolded on the Sea Islands, many once altruistic Gideonites acquired reputations as "nothing now but speculators."[14] Like Iraq, the Port Royal Experiment failed to fulfill its potential of paying for itself, and if components of Iraq and Afghanistan became an ambiguous mix of national security, humanitarianism, and profit, Willie Lee Rose laments that many Gideonites also saw their work as a hybrid "philanthropic-commercial venture."[15]

Contrabands preparing cotton for the gin on Smith's plantation on Port Royal Island in 1862. Courtesy Library of Congress Prints and Photographs Division Washington, DC.

Indeed, Rose notes a certain element of economic imperialism permeating the Port Royal Experiment.[16] American domination of the world market for raw cotton was at the time threatened by expanded production in Egypt; Asia Minor; Brazil; and, particularly, India. Government officials like Chase could not help but note increased cotton exports would build up favorable foreign exchange that would facilitate payment of the public debt held abroad, finance increased imports, support specie payment, and combat inflation.[17] Decisions about local economic development on the Sea Islands would not be made independently of national economic considerations, and certainly the government hoped to reap strategic benefits from its tactical efforts.

The Individual

Along with these competing motivations, Robert Chambers convincingly argues that "any development agenda is value-laden," and the case of the Port Royal Experiment is no exception.[18] Convinced of the moral and economic superiority of their native North, the Gideonites wholeheartedly expected the Sea Islands blacks to embrace enthusiastically the free-labor ideology and its emphasis on economic independence through wage earning. The Gideonites seemed genuinely surprised that the freedmen instead desired to operate a sustainable subsistence economy on their own homelands.[19]

Reflecting the Enlightenment philosophy that attached happiness to other notions such as progress and prosperity, the Gideonites championed an economic course they thought would best generate this outcome.[20] In this regard they have plenty of more modern company. Rory Stewart blames the flawed American modernization effort in Vietnam on "a materialist worldview whose gods were technology and progress, which denied the reality of cultural difference."[21] The South Vietnamese peasants and the black Sea Islanders viewed happiness in other contexts, and subsequent observers, including Richard Easterlin, Jared Diamond, and Tony Waters, also have noted that happiness cannot uniformly be measured in material terms.[22] Representing these arguments, Vandana Shiva explains, "Culturally perceived poverty need not be real material poverty: subsistence economies which serve basic needs through self-provisioning are not poor in the sense of being deprived." The danger she continues, is that "the ideology of development declares them so."[23]

Developmental efforts on the Sea Islands followed this conventional wisdom, although for many of the former slaves, freedom was a much more powerful motivation than economic development. For whatever prosperity cotton promised, these new freedmen saw the crop as inexorably tied to slavery and working for a master rather than themselves. They understood freedom as owning their own land, farming it as they pleased, and living largely independent of the market place. Growing vegetables and selling fish to the soldiers was a much preferable alternative to raising cotton for wages.[24]

For these former slaves, being free meant more than merely being paid. It meant being able "to take control of the conditions under which they labored, free themselves from subordination to white authority, and carve out the greatest measure of economic autonomy."[25] When Abram Murcherson was asked in January 1865, "What will [the former slaves] do when the War is over?," he replied, "Go out into the land and make their homes there. Buy 20 acres of land. This is what should be: once settled on his 20 acres, no one can oppress the negro hereafter. But without land all the teaching, all the philanthropy, all the Christianity of the world cannot save him from the oppression of his selfish neighbor who holds the means of bread in his own hands."[26] According to this understanding, the principal measure of the happiness associated with individual economic development was freedom, not wealth. Critical to this notion of freedom, and the security and happiness it implied, was the land ownership that could come only from land reform. Abbott summarizes, "As one of their most cherished dreams, the great majority of ex-slaves longed for ownership of the soil; to them 'forty acres and a mule' symbolized the essence of liberty."[27]

Such individual preferences did not rank high on the government's economic plan. Hermine Baumhofer puts the priorities in focus, writing, "The occupying forces wanted the land under production; the cotton for which the North had dire need, had to be sowed and harvested. It was hoped that the Negro could be provided for in these necessary activities with which he was familiar."[28] Thus, LaWanda Cox argues that the "primary interest" guiding all policy decisions about land disposition "was the restoration and expansion of cotton culture."[29] If somehow the interests and aspirations of the black Sea Islanders were met in the process, such would be a welcome outcome, but it certainly was not the dominant criterion.

Land Policy and Reform

This prioritization had significant ramifications across the socio-economic spectrum as various parties worked to develop a land policy. In many respects, the basic positions were mutually exclusive, and Akiko Ochiai describes the Port Royal Experiment as being caught between the desire of the black population to own land and the Northern capitalists' vision of the freedmen as cheap wage labor.[30] More was at stake in the resolution of this conflict than mere economic development. As Solon Barraclough notes, "Land reform is primarily an issue of basic human rights. It implies access to land and its benefits on more equitable and secure terms for all of those who physically work it and primarily depend upon it for their livelihoods."[31] The tension between various interpretations of the purpose of land reform, as well as the interests of the diverse stakeholders, made the disposition of land abandoned by the Sea Islands' white population a complicated and controversial matter.

Many Gideonites championed black land ownership, but for a variety of reasons. Reuben Tomlinson viewed the issue as one of entitlement and restitution, arguing that "if there is any class of people in the country who have priority of claim to the confiscated lands of the South, it certainly is that class who have by years of suffering and unrequited toil given to these lands any value they may now possess."[32] Tomlinson's view is consistent with Barraclough's assertion that "in unjust agrarian structures," land should be redistributed "to benefit the landless and near landless at the expense of large landholders and others who appropriated most of its benefits before reform."[33] Pierce also advocated black land ownership, but with a purpose at least in part justified by the free-labor ideology. He proposed that the freedmen "should have the power to acquire the fee simple of land, either with the proceeds of their labor or as a reward of special merit; and it would be well to quicken their zeal for good behavior by proper recognitions."[34] Pierce's view ignores Barraclough's interpretation of access to land as a basic human right and instead considers it a privilege to be earned by conformity to externally determined norms.

Other Northerners were even stricter in their devotion to the free-labor ideology, seeming to be genuinely surprised the former slaves aspired to become landowners rather than willingly work the cotton plantations as wage laborers.[35] Fearing economic self-determination would lead only "to idle and thriftless habits," Gideonites like Edward Philbrick, who would ultimately become the principal land and labor overseer of the Port Royal Experiment, believed the discipline learned by wage earning would benefit the blacks not just materially, but morally as well.[36] William Gannett concurred, believing it would be "most unwise and injurious" to give the blacks free lands when they could become "more intelligent, . . . more industrious and persistent" by working to obtain them. Instead, he argued, "Let all the natural laws of labor, wages, competition &c come into play,— and the sooner will habits of responsibility, industry, self-dependence & manliness be developed."[37]

In the process, the blacks would become consumers that would fuel the national economy. Pennsylvanian James McKim saw the Port Royal freedmen as "ten thousand new customers." If the black population could be transitioned to productive wage earners, they would soon demand "pots, kettles, pans, brushes, brooms, knives, forks, spoons, soap, candles, combs, Yankee clocks, etc. etc" that could be provided by northern manufacture. A staunch abolitionist, McKim could recognize "an overwhelming economical argument" for freedom as well as the obvious moral one.[38] Gideonite Austa French concurred, writing, "Imagine the trade set in motion the moment they get wages. What a brisk market for everything conceivable."[39] Rose concludes this "vision of a freed people as agricultural peasants devoted to a single-crop economy and educated to a taste for consumer goods supplied by Northern factories fulfills the classic pattern of tributary economies the world over."[40]

With such competing ideas, the disposition of the land left abandoned when the white population fled the Sea Islands was no easy matter. Under the Direct Tax Act of June 1862, if the owner failed to pay his taxes, the U.S. government could seize the property for either rent or sale at auction. With this purpose in mind, three tax commissioners arrived on the Sea Islands in

October 1862 and announced that land sales would be held in February 1863. Fearing most of the land would go to rich northern speculators rather than freedmen, Saxton succeeded in convincing Congress to set aside a portion of the land for military and charitable uses and postpone the sale of the remaining lands until March. Under these revised procedures, black Sea Islanders were able to purchase some two thousand acres; a small victory, but nothing compared to the eight thousand acres that ended up under the control of Philbrick.[41]

Philbrick was a thirty-four year old who, Rose claims, came to Port Royal "at considerable personal sacrifice."[42] Leaving behind his family and well-established career as an engineer and architect in Boston, Philbrick sailed for Port Royal with the first contingent of Gideonites in March 1862. Gannett considered Philbrick "one of the most valuable men" in the group.[43] Pierce also recognized Philbrick's capabilities, making him superintendent of the large district centered around the Coffin Point plantation where Philbrick would have to contend with the intransigence of cotton agent Colonel William Nobles.[44]

Rose considers Philbrick "the one evangel who thought hard about economics" and "the ablest businessman on the islands."[45] Shaped by free-labor ideology and the classical capitalist approach to economic development, Philbrick's natural solution to development on the Sea Islands was to continue to raise cotton using the plantation system modified by substituting wage for slave labor.[46] Well aware of the challenges posed by the two-month delay in planting, pests, and other obstacles, he shrugged off the low yields of the first year and roundly praised the black labor force.[47] Indeed, Philbrick had fared better than his fellow missionary-planters that first year, in part because he had acquiesced to the freedmen's demand to organize labor by the familiar task system rather than in gangs controlled by a driver. Under the task system, Philbrick placed "each family on its own responsibility, assigning to each a definite portion of land and allowing them to choose their own time and manner of working it."[48] The result was that Philbrick had turned a small profit in spite of all the difficulties.

The main obstacle Philbrick saw to even greater gains was government control.[49] A staunch advocate of laissez-faire, Philbrick proposed a plan for private ownership that would allow him "to continue this free-labor experiment through a term of years and under circumstances more favorable than those under which we have this year been placed."[50] He shared his idea with John Murray Forbes who on January 21, 1863, informed Philbrick that Forbes could raise twelve thousand dollars to be used to purchase land and for other operating costs. The result was that on April 8, Philbrick and fourteen businessmen, including Forbes, agreed to form a consortium. Philbrick would buy the land in his name, assume complete responsibility for its management, and be liable for all losses. For his efforts, he would receive one-fourth of the net profits, after paying the subscribers 6 percent interest. The subscribers could not withdraw their investment so long as Philbrick continued as manager, nor could Philbrick request additional contributions. When the business closed, the proceeds would be divided pro rata.[51]

To the chagrin of many missionaries who favored black land ownership, when the first land sales occurred on March 9, Philbrick and his joint-stock company bought eleven cotton plantations, totaling eight thousand acres and leased two others from the government. For a mere seven thousand dollars, Philbrick and his partners had gained possession of one-third of St. Helena Island and indirect control over the nearly one thousand people who lived there.[52] As a result, many of the old plantations merely passed into private hands still in plantation units.[53] Furthermore, "first-string Gideonites" such as Gannett and Charles Ware soon resigned from their positions as government superintendents to manage Philbrick's plantations.[54]

While many missionaries immediately accused Philbrick of acting only in his self-interest, his disposition is consistent with the capitalist approach to economic development, which favors the concentration of capital as a way of spurring investment rather than consumption.[55] Such a strategy helps realize economies of scale and promotes specialization, leading economists such as Edward Atkinson to argue the freedmen should focus on cotton and buy western grains.[56] It also prevents the fragmentation that threatens efficiency. Thus, Philbrick cautioned, "Anyone who has watched the minute subdivision of lands among the

French peasantry knows that after a few generations a man has not land enough to live on or work economically, and hence a vast amount of time and energy is wasted in France for lack of organization."[57]

Another goal of the capitalist model is to tie development to the world economy and international trade.[58] Concentration would produce more and cheaper cotton, and more and cheaper cotton would give New England manufacturers a share in the markets of India and China and larger sales at home. As McKim and French appreciated, this vigorous cotton economy would also increase the market for northern products in the South.[59] The result would be an updated version of the antebellum triangular trade system.

This capitalist vision of concentration was threatened when a second land sale of forty thousand acres was scheduled for the fall. Under these proceedings, some sixteen thousand acres were to be divided into twenty-acre plots reserved for blacks at a price of $1.25 per acre. This provision delighted advocates of a land redistribution policy to benefit landless freedmen, especially when Saxton announced a policy of preemption. As practiced on the western frontier since the 1840s, preemption entitled those who had improved and settled on surveyed and public lands the first rights of purchase at a fixed price when the lands were offered at public auction. Now Saxton instructed Sea Islands blacks wishing to purchase disposed lands at the next sale to describe the plots they desired and make cash deposits for them at his headquarters. By the end of January 1864, blacks had claimed six thousand acres according to these procedures.[60]

Ardent preemptionists argued that the policy responded to a national obligation to remediate past injustices to the slaves.[61] Frederick Williams expressed this sentiment, asking, "Shall we, who owe the race so heavy a debt, dash this hope to the earth, and leave the debt unpaid?"[62] Likening the initiative to what "in today's context . . . looks like an affirmative action program intended to give the disadvantaged the wherewithal to step up to the starting line in a competitive society," Akiko Ochiai declares the preemption argument "a revolutionary concept of justice," given the nineteenth century understanding of equality.[63] In many ways it reflected the socialist argument that economic development includes a more equitable distribution of wealth as well as Barraclough's assertion that "land reform without the state's participation would be a contradiction of terms."[64] For Ochiai, this state participation would take the form of some "affirmative mechanism for correcting the excesses of big moneyed interests and unbridled capitalism."[65] Finally, socialism's belief that improving the position of the poor should happen "sooner rather than later" stands in sharp contrast to Philbrick's concern that "it will not be well" for the freedmen "to make money so fast on their cotton and land."[66] Absent some means of addressing these considerations, Ochiai pronounced the goal of a more egalitarian society "doomed to failure."[67]

On the other hand, anti-preemptionists, while acknowledging the moral bankruptcy of slavery, saw grave danger in violating the central principles of the market. Selling land below market value and denying equal access to all prospective buyers only added to the past injustices. It also warred against the free-labor ideology, which linked "demoralization" to assumption of unearned privileges.[68] "No man," explained Philbrick, "appreciates property who does not work for it, on the same terms with those around him."[69] In countering this logic with the remediation argument, Eric Foner notes Philbrick "failed to consider the possibility that the former slaves had worked for the land during their 250 years of bondage."[70]

With even the Gideonites split on the issue and confusion abounding, Secretary Chase reversed the preemption policy and announced in mid-February 1864 that black Sea Islanders would in fact have to bid against other buyers.[71] The result was "a veritable free-for-all," with speculators driving prices up from one dollar to as much as twenty-seven dollars per acre.[72] "We are nothing now but speculators," bemoaned Gannett, "and the righteous rail against us."[73] Under these new rules, when the sale was conducted on February 18, most tracts were sold to northern whites for more than eleven dollars per acre. President Lincoln, however, had held firm on the provision to reserve sixteen thousand acres, and as a small consolation, 110 black families managed to buy parcels of this land at the $1.25 per acre price.[74]

The hope of land reform advocates was renewed when Major General William Sherman issued Special Field Order No. 15 on January 16, 1865. This dramatic act seized as federal property "the islands from Charleston, south, the abandoned rice fields along the rivers for thirty miles back from the sea, and the country bordering the St. Johns River, Florida," and reserved them "for the settlement of the negroes now made free by the acts of war and the proclamation of the President of the United States."[75] Because Sherman's decision was based more on military pragmatics than a long-term social program, it did not represent a deliberate component of economic development and proved to not be a permanent policy. Eager to rebuild the nation peacefully, President Johnson issued an Amnesty Proclamation on May 29, 1865, that allowed former Confederates to be pardoned and have their confiscated lands returned to them. In spite of the efforts of the Freedmen's Bureau's Major General Oliver Howard and other advocates of black land ownership, this policy eventually came to include even the land in "Sherman's reserve." By late February and early March, U.S. Army units were forcibly returning lands to their former owners and making freedmen sign labor contracts or leave.[76]

The terms of the contracts varied, but they generally involved some version of sharecropping. While the contracts helped establish the principle that blacks now had certain rights and privileges, it was a system "far short of perfection." As a result, Abbott concludes, it left "the great majority of Negro workers ... hardly any better off materially than they had been under slavery."[77]

Political processes, like the one that determined land and labor policy on the Sea Islands, are often viewed as means of making decisions about the distribution of finite resources.[78] This equation is especially pronounced in an agricultural society where land is the basic factor of production. Because the supply of land is finite, "the landlord loses what the peasant acquires."[79] Any discussion of land reform will be a particularly contentious political process because such a zero-sum game may result in "a change in power relationships in favor of those who physically work the land at the expense of those who primarily accumulate wealth from their control over rural land and labor."[80] Barraclough

argues that the state, as the "institutionalized political organization of society," plays a critical role in land reform by articulating and implementing public policy and adjudicating conflicts.[81]
Based on this understanding, reform did not occur on the Sea
Islands and elsewhere because of insufficient state commitment
to comprehensive economic change. Senator Charles Sumner
had predicted as much, insisting that Reconstruction "would be
incomplete unless in some way we secured to the freedmen a
piece of land."[82] To Sumner's chagrin, the final result was a series
of half-measures, with advocates of what they called a New South
acknowledging the need to find a replacement for slave labor but
with "no intention of seeing the finest land in the region fall into
black hands."[83]

Even more specifically, Foner explains the lack of significant economic development in the postwar South as being the
result of a failure "to come to grips with the plantation system
itself." He argues that "throughout the world, plantation societies are characterized by persistent economic backwardness."
Planter classes, whether the old slaveholding aristocracy or the
new breed represented by Philbrick, "use their political power to
prevent the emergence of alternative economic enterprises that
might threaten their control of the labor force." The failure to
inaugurate serious land reform on the Sea Islands is an example
of leadership that Foner asserts merely "wanted the trappings of
economic development without accepting its full implications—
an agrarian revolution and a free labor market."[84] Genuine land
reform would have involved "a fundamental reordering of power
and status, a reordering of the basic social relationship," which
was more than the government was willing to impose.[85]

Gap Hypothesis

Such immediate reform is not inherent in the capitalist development strategy that defers equity in order to maximize efficiency.
Instead, the planned course is to have the state redress poverty
and other social ills only after a self-sustaining cycle of accumu-
lation is under way.[86] Following this model, the orchestrators of

the Port Royal Experiment decided black aspirations for land ownership would have to wait, in the process unleashing "a deep and sullen anger" among the freedmen.[87]

Rose notes "the Northerners understood but did not view with sufficient sympathy" the black Sea Islanders' frustration with their inability to procure land.[88] Like any other experiment, the one at Port Royal would be judged by results, and when the Gideonites began reviewing their work, they tended to focus on areas other than land ownership. Today's nation builders also rely on measures of effectiveness (MOEs) "to assess changes in system behavior, capability, or operational environment that [are] tied to measuring the attainment of an end state, achievement of an objective, or creation of an effect."[89] When Pierce considered the progress on the Sea Islands in 1865, he turned to MOEs attesting to "the evidences of prosperity that have accumulated in the homes of Port Royal." Citing such factors as new homes that had been built; old homes that had been repaired or enlarged; fences that had been constructed; wood chimneys that had been replaced by brick ones; farm animals, wagons, furniture, and kitchen utensils that had been acquired; and improvements in dress and diet, Pierce spoke glowingly of the gains the blacks had made.[90] He bragged that "every family has its private 'nest egg' laid by for a land sale," but he seemingly ignored the lack of opportunity for the blacks to apply these savings toward the cherished purchase.[91] In fact, the South Carolina Savings Bank at Beaufort, which was established in 1864 in hopes of teaching freedmen the "habits of carefulness and prudence," did not finance a single head right purchase in spite of leading the public to believe it had loaned out money for the purchase of twenty-acre farms, such as the ones set aside by Sherman's Special Field Order No. 15. While it is possible some accounts had already been settled, not a single freedman homestead was among the loans outstanding on the books of the Beaufort Branch when it closed its doors in 1873.[92] In ignoring the frustration blacks felt at being deprived of opportunities to own land, Pierce fell into the common trap of relying on tangible MOEs rather than the more important but harder to quantify factors such as personal satisfaction and commitment.[93] Given that Pierce set out at least in part to prepare the freedmen "for useful and worthy citizenship," he seems remiss in not more earnestly attempting to capture the social and interpersonal variables associated with this end state.[94]

By discounting the importance of landownership to the blacks' vision of their own economic development, the Gideonites became agnostic of what Samuel Huntington identifies as the gap that can develop "between aspiration and expectation, want formation, and want satisfaction, or the aspirations function and the level-of-living function." The problem, according to Huntington, is that "the ability of transitional society to satisfy . . . new aspirations . . . increases much more slowly than the aspirations themselves."[95] During his first visit to the Sea Islands, Pierce had promised the freedmen "that by-and-by they would be as well off as the white people."[96] For those who had been so long enslaved, the desire for change was a little more urgent, yet many Gideonites saw the black protests against the slow pace of progress as "simply signs of ingratitude."[97]

The awakening that accompanies exposure to new possibilities is difficult to reverse. One freedman explained that "he had lived all his life with a basket over his head, and now that it had been taken off and air and sunlight had come to him, he could not consent to have the basket over him again."[98] When such individuals are denied the opportunities they have come to expect, they become frustrated and dissatisfied. Political instability, at a level commensurate with the extent of the gap between aspiration and reality, is the likely result.[99] On the Sea Islands, these unrealized wants manifested themselves in black challenges to the failure of land reform and the imposition of wage contracts.

Gannett observed that after the failure of preemption, the black population was left "unsettled, discontented, and grumbling." Some, he reported, "refuse to have anything to do with the new proprietors."[100] Expressing a common sentiment, one freedman said, "If a man got to go crost de riber, and he can't git a boat, he take a log. If I can't own de land, I'll hire or lease it . . . , but I won't contract."[101] Small acts of disobedience soon surfaced such as planting corn instead of cotton, leaving Gannett to confess, "The truth is here,— that we are rather more in the power of the negroes than they in ours."[102] When William Allen chastised the freedmen for misappropriating Philbrick's property by planting corn, one responded, "Man! Don't talk 'bout Mr. Philbrick lan'. Mr. Philbrick no right to de lan'."[103] Such arguments, however, were of little practical value against armed soldiers who compelled the blacks to sign contracts or leave. Some blacks, presumably mostly among the original refugees from Georgia, did opt to go, but the majority was forced to accept the fact that with spring at hand, "nature called men, white or black, to plant or starve."[104]

The result was a condition that left no party fully satisfied, and every group suspicious of the other.[105] As predicted by Huntington's gap hypothesis, instability abounded. Such a situation of incomplete revolution, unfulfilled aspirations, and unresolved issues of power would inevitably lead to continued conflict. In the immediate situation, the Freedmen's Bureau was ill-equipped to deal with such challenges to the fragile peace, and in the long term, the United States was unwilling to deepen and perpetuate its commitment by creating the "neo-trusteeship" that James Fearon and David Laitin argue such conditions require.[106] As a result, the white southern population was better able to manipulate the instability to its advantage and recapture economic dominance on the Sea Islands.

Half-Results from Half-Measures

Tryon Edwards, an American theologian at the time of the Port Royal Experiment, observed that "compromise is but the sacrifice of one right or good in the hope of retaining another—too often ending in the loss of both," and the effort to balance the competing socioeconomic stresses on the Sea Islands bears testimony to Edwards's caution.[107] Rose laments that "few of the promised blessings of progress had followed" the effort "to create a great commercial center on the islands."[108] With Sea Island cotton production dropping from 54,904 bales during the three years before the war to just 23,307 bales between 1870 and 1873, northern dreams of the "expansion of cotton culture" had been unrealized.[109] Visionaries who sought increased land ownership were also disappointed. In his study of St. Helena's Parish,

Hermann Baumhofer finds of the 121 individuals who described themselves as planters and farmers in St. Helena Parish in 1860, 111 owned land. Even the ten planters without land, he surmises, were the younger sons on their father's plantations. In 1870, the census shows that 1,933 individuals described themselves as farmers and planters but that only 957 of them owned land. With 50 percent of the farmers now landless, tenancy rather than ownership was the new norm. Also, the value of the land had been reduced almost by half between 1860 and 1870.[110] The collapse of the slave aristocracy had certainly resulted in disproportionate wealth never again being concentrated in the hands of so few, but at that same time, the overall standard of living had sharply declined.[111] The Port Royal Experiment may have increased economic equality, but it did not bring the hoped for economic prosperity.

CHAPTER EIGHT

Political Development and Democratization

If the Prussian military theorist Carl von Clausewitz is correct in saying "war is the continuation of policy by other means," the thoughtful and deliberate determination of that policy would seem to be central.[1] Instead, the Federal policy involving both the objective of the Civil War and the objective of Reconstruction evolved over time, with the latter appearing particularly underdeveloped. At first President Abraham Lincoln insisted on a limited war objective of restoring the Union. In an August 22, 1862, letter to newspaper editor Horace Greeley, Lincoln explained, "My paramount object in this struggle is to save the Union, and is not either to save or to destroy slavery. If I could save the Union without freeing any slave I would do it, and if I could save it by freeing all the slaves I would do it; and if I could save it by freeing some and leaving others alone I would also do that."[2] It was not until the Emancipation Proclamation went into effect on January 1, 1863, that abolition was added as a paramount goal of the war effort.

The objective of Reconstruction also changed from the vision of "with malice toward none, with charity for all . . . to bind up the nation's wounds" espoused by Lincoln in his March 4, 1865 second inaugural address and practiced through the conciliatory and limited approach of Andrew Johnson's Presidential Reconstruction to a much more punitive and transformational venture under the Congressional Reconstruction engineered by the Radical Republicans. In these contexts, the northern war aim can be analyzed as beginning as one primarily focused on national security and later assuming some of the characteristics of more recent efforts at liberal interventionism. Likewise, Reconstruction can be understood as moving from a simple restoration of peace with only the bare essential challenges to the status quo to a much more ambitious effort to build liberal democracy.

Presidential and Congressional Reconstruction

The process of democratization has attracted much practical and theoretical attention in the post–Cold War era, and a variety of scholars have examined U.S. and international efforts to promote democratic reform, especially after military intervention. Roland Paris argues that one component of these reforms should be an electoral system that helps promote reconciliation among former adversaries by rewarding moderation. He notes one way of affecting this outcome is to embed such incentives in the state constitution.[3] Such an opportunity first presented itself in post–Civil War South Carolina at the state constitutional convention that met on September 13, 1865.

Reflecting the expectations that emerged after the Federal victory, "a large meeting of freedmen, held on St. Helena Island" on September 4, petitioned "the Convention about to be assembled at Columbia, on the 13th instant, to so alter and amend the present Constitution of this State as to give the right of suffrage to every man of the age of twenty-one years, without other qualifications than that required for the white citizens of this State."[4] The meeting and the resolution were reported without the dignity of elaboration in the *Columbia Daily Phoenix* on September 23, ten days after the opening of the state convention the freedmen had intended to influence. The convention showed similar indifference to such sentiments. Indeed, in his instructions to the convention members, Benjamin Perry, a prewar unionist and proponent of slavery, appointed provisional governor by President Johnson, noted,

> The radical Republican party [members of the] North are looking with great interest to the action of the Southern States in reference to negro suffrage, and whilst they admit that a man should

be able to read and write and have property qualification in order to vote, yet they contend that there should be no distinction between voters on account of color. They forget that this is a white man's government, and intended for white men only; and that the Supreme Court of the United States has decided that the negro is not an American citizen under the Federal Constitution. That each and every State of the Union has the unquestioned right of deciding for herself who shall exercise the right of suffrage is beyond all dispute. You will settle this grave question as the interest and Honor of the State demand.[5]

Taking their cues from the limited demands President Johnson imposed, Perry and the state convention continued South Carolina's prewar defiance of federal authority. Ignoring or downplaying requirements such as "unqualified abolition," declaring secession "null and void," and repudiating Confederate debt, the convention set out to solidify white control of the state. A key component in this effort was to draft a code for the "regulation of labor and the protection and government of the colored population of the State."[6] The result was a Black Code that "clearly indicated the future of Carolina society should whites remain in control."[7]

Instead, the code delivered a "chilling object lesson in the restraints" imposed upon any "self-generated change" by white Southerners and forced federal action. Having no intention of leaving the matter in the hands of the South Carolinians' "deeply ingrained intellectual, ideological, and racial assumptions," the Thirty-ninth Congress, upon convening in December, refused to seat the state's and other southern representatives.[8] Arguing that President Johnson had exceeded his presidential authority, the Republican majority created a Joint Committee on Reconstruction that would determine new, less conciliatory practices by which the former Confederate states would be restored to the Union. As a result of this new agenda, on June 13, 1866, Congress passed the Fourteenth Amendment, which declared that "all persons born or naturalized in the United States . . . are citizens of the United States" and guaranteed such citizens "due process of law." It also contained provisions that presented officeholding disabilities and disfranchisement for many white Southerners and established incentives for states either to grant black voting rights or proportionally lose representation in Congress.

Posed with this challenge to his interpretation of "the interest and Honor of the State," Governor Perry took his case to several northern newspapers. To the *New York Tribune* he warned that "if the negro will be invested with all political power, then the antagonism of interests between capital and labor is to work out the final result" and to the *New York Herald* he boasted "that the people of South Carolina have honor and sagacity enough to reject with scorn and indignation this constitutional amendment."[9] He lectured the *Tribune*'s readers that "this Government has been the white man's government, both federal and state. It was formed by white men and for white men exclusively."[10] The paper begged to differ, accusing Perry of wanting to "put the clock four years back" which they assured him was "impossible." Instead, "South Carolina must present herself at the doors of the House next December with words quite other than his on her repentant lips, if she looks to see those doors fly open to her delegation."[11]

This struggle between federal and state authority proved to be much more than a rhetorical one. The Reconstruction Act of 1867 placed the South under military occupation, dividing it into five military districts commanded by officers empowered to use the army to "protect all persons in their rights of person and property, to suppress insurrection, disorder, and violence, and to punish, or cause to be punished, all disturbers of the public peace and criminals." The act also stated that the former Confederate states would not be "declared entitled to representation in Congress" until they ratified "a constitution of government in conformity with the Constitution of the United States in all respects, framed by a convention of delegates elected by the male citizens of said State, twenty-one years old and upward, of whatever race, color, or previous condition" and ratified the Fourteenth Amendment.

These developments represented a marked shift in the federal government's approach and the fate of South Carolina. Whereas previous efforts had focused "on influencing, conciliating, and cajoling the white population," the Reconstruction Act "placed the focus on the voting population at large, including the black portion of it."[12] Most states with large black populations accepted the inevitable and responded by trying to elect conservatives to their upcoming convention. South Carolina took the opposite approach and attempted a "register and reject" strategy. Conservatives hoped to swell the roles by registering in large numbers and then boycotting or voting "no" at the election in order to sabotage the requirement that for a convention to be held, a majority of those registered had to vote for it. The tactic nearly worked, but by a slim margin a convention was assembled in Charleston on January 14, 1868. Of the 124 delegates, 73 were black, 36 were southern whites who were nearly all Republicans, and the remainder were carpetbagger whites from the North. By the middle of March, a new constitution, which included the required provision for impartial male suffrage, was ready, and elections were held in April. Robert Scott, who had succeeded Saxton as the Freedmen's Bureau's assistant commissioner for the states of South Carolina, Georgia, and Florida, was elected governor. Along with him, nearly the entire Republican ticket was elected, and the new constitution also passed. It was quickly accepted by Congress, and in June, South Carolina was readmitted to the Union.[13]

While these results displaced the former white elite rule and opened up unprecedented black political representation and power, they also presented serious problems. The first was that the newly elected officials, as a group, lacked experience with, and in many cases qualification for, their new responsibilities. Their ability to govern effectively was far from certain. Secondly, the vast majority of South Carolina whites rejected the idea of black political power and considered the new government and any actions it might attempt to be illegitimate. As a result, conservative whites would mount an organized campaign to resist this turn of events. Finally, the irony of the Republican victory was that with it came an assumption of progress that led to a reduction of the presence and activity of both the U.S. Army and the Freedmen's Bureau. South Carolina's Republican government, hamstrung by its own limitations and opposed by a still powerful section of the population, would have to face these challenges largely alone.[14]

Black Political Leadership

The ouster of South Carolina's white leadership was one thing. Replacing it would be another. The antebellum slave experience simply had not afforded opportunities for blacks to hone political or leadership skills. Simon Bolivar, the Liberator of Latin America, faced a similar situation earlier in the century, explaining, "The role of the inhabitants of the American hemisphere has for centuries been purely passive. Politically they were nonexistent. We are still in a position lower than slavery, and therefore it is more difficult for us to rise to the enjoyment of freedom.... We have been harassed by a conduct which has not only deprived us of our rights but has kept us in a sort of permanent infancy with regard to public affairs. If we could at least have managed our domestic affairs and our internal administration, we could have acquainted ourselves with the processes and mechanics of public affairs."[15] Although committed to the democratic ideals of the Enlightenment, the newly independent countries of Latin American simply lacked the necessary experience to put them into practice.

A similar situation unfolded in South Carolina, where the reversal of political power had come because "with Republican help, an inexperienced mass of former slaves had mobilized, unified, and seized the future."[16] While such an assessment has great populist appeal, it represented only a beginning of the difficult task that lay ahead and, as in Latin America, in no way ensured success. As it turned out, the government that came to power in South Carolina in 1867 was plagued by an understandable shortage of qualified black leaders and by the selfish motives of many of the white carpetbaggers. There were, however, exceptions.

The most fertile proving ground for black political development was the site of the Port Royal Experiment, where the Gideonites had sought to "create a model society" and begin the Sea Islanders on the path to self-government through the vehicle of the New England–style town meeting.[17] During this "political incubation period," signs of increased black interest in politics began to materialize in the forms of secret oaths, ceremonies, emblems, songs, and other appeals to emotion. Union Leagues and similar groups attracted great followings that brought together Freedmen's Bureau agents, black soldiers, and local freedmen united in the cause of black suffrage and political education. A meeting in St. Helena in 1865 voiced the representative sentiment that "by the Declaration of Independence we believe these are rights which cannot be denied us." It was out of these embryonic stages of political consciousness that Robert Smalls emerged as the area's most enduring black political leader.[18]

Smalls first attracted national attention on May 13, 1862 during the siege of Charleston when, as a twenty-three year old slave impressed into duties as pilot of the Confederate *Planter*, he escaped with the ship and its black crew members into the Federal blockade lines. Smalls brought with him news that the Confederates had abandoned their positions guarding the seaward approaches to James Island, leaving Charleston vulnerable to an attack from the rear across the island. While the resulting Federal attempted coup de main to seize Charleston was a dismal failure, Smalls was elevated to the status of a hero. He also received $1,500 in prize money for delivering the Confederate vessel to Federal authorities.[19]

The *Planter*, along with Smalls, then entered into federal service. After participating in a minor expedition to test Confederate defenses up the North Edisto River in June, Smalls was transferred to Admiral Samuel DuPont's flagship *Wabash* to serve as pilot. He was often called away from military service, however, to serve as a spokesman on behalf of the Port Royal Experiment.[20] For example, he and Mansfield French traveled to Washington and met with Secretary of War Edwin Stanton on August 20, 1862, to discuss options for enlisting blacks in the army.[21] Throughout the duration of the war, Smalls continued to mix military service and advocacy work on behalf of the freedmen. The experience left him well-postured to "transform wartime fame into political power."[22]

In spite of Smalls having been part of an unprecedented effort to send a black delegation to the National Union Convention that met in Baltimore, Maryland, on June 7, 1864, his biographer, Edward Miller, notes that he maintained a "seemingly low political profile during the early postwar period."[23] Nonetheless, this

Robert Smalls as he appeared in the 1870s. Courtesy Library of Congress
Prints and Photographs Division Washington, DC.

period was critical to the preparation of Smalls for his future
role. Even before he entered politics, Smalls was "demonstrating
community leadership" in a variety of ways.[24] As such, he represents the emergence of new leadership necessary to the ability to
hold elections in a nation building effort.[25]

L. Earnest Sellers declared Smalls's "rise to political importance in South Carolina during Reconstruction [to have been]

inevitable."[26] In addition to the fame gained by his delivery of the *Planter* and other wartime service, Smalls had become economically independent and was reportedly "able to give bread to half the bank presidents and brokers of Broad St. [Charleston]."[27] Biographer Andrew Billingsley credits this "entrepreneurial base" to Smalls's formative experience as one of the "favored house servants" of Henry McKee.[28] Billingsley describes the kind McKee as "a substitute father figure" who taught Smalls "some rudimentary skills in management" as part of his household duties.[29] Not surprising, Thomas Holt finds that many of South Carolina's early black political leaders came from a similar slave background as an artisan or house servant.[30] The socialization advantages of such an experience when contrasted with those of a field hand are obvious.

The positive relationship between Smalls and McKee continued after the war when the fortunes of the two men had largely been reversed. Smalls bought the destitute McKee a house and did numerous favors for the McKee family that included taking an old and infirm Mrs. McKee into his home after her husband's death. Smalls's kind treatment of the McKees earned him the respect of the white community and made him "to the whites the least objectionable of the freedmen with political aspirations."[31] His moderate and conciliatory stance was for whites a welcome contrast to the threat posed by those postconflict electoral winners who emerge "dedicated to the violent destruction of their rivals."[32]

White Resistance

A man of Smalls's characteristics is exactly what is required of a consociational approach to power sharing after a military intervention. This technique attempts to manage internal divisions along ethnic, religious, linguistic, racial, or other lines by consultation among the elites of each of the society's major social groups.[33] Confederate cavalry hero and planter Wade Hampton represented a possible counterpart on the white side. While questioning President Johnson's legal authority to compel states to hold constitutional conventions, Hampton conceded that

Johnson had such a right as a "conqueror." Hampton advised his fellow whites they were obligated to accept Washington's "terms" and were "bound, by every dictate of honor and manliness, to abide by them honestly and to keep, in good faith, the pledges you have given." Certainly, Hampton's moderation was largely pragmatic, and his desire was certainly to control rather than empower the black electorate, but he still was willing to make concessions and compromises. To a national Democratic leader who advocated a more conservative stance, Hampton wrote

> If we cannot direct the wave it will overwhelm us. Now how
> shall we do this? Simply by making the Negro a Southern Man,
> & if you will, a democrat, anything but a Radical. Beyond these
> motives for my actions, I have another. We are appealing to the
> enlightened sense & the justice of mankind. We come forward &
> say, we accept the decision rendered against us, we acknowledge
> the freedom of the negro & we are willing to have our love for
> him stir us. We are making up our record for posterity & we wish
> no blemish or flaw to be found there.[34]

Hampton's message resonated with many blacks, including Beverly Nash, an influential senator from Richland County whom Hampton reciprocally declared "respectable" and "true."[35] "Why should we not be friends?," Hampton asked a black audience. "Are you not Southern men, as we are? Is this not your home as well as ours? Does not the glorious Southern sun above us shine alike for both of us? Did not this soil give birth to all of us?"[36] Even black nationalist Martin Delaney, "perhaps the most respected black leader in the state," would come to endorse Hampton in the 1876 gubernatorial race, believing it was in the best interest of the black race to work with former supporters of the Confederacy.[37] In seemingly consociational fashion, "Hampton and other elites held out hope of a partnership between white and black elites," but, continues Hampton's biographer Rod Andrew, it was one designed to "control the black vote and preserve elite white leadership."[38]

The root problem was that even Smalls's moderation was intolerable to most of South Carolina's conservative white population.

A *Harper's Weekly* engraving from 1867 sarcastically depicting the "New Era" of South Carolina politics with Hampton and a former slave courteously reconciled. Courtesy Library of Congress Prints and Photographs Division Washington, DC.

Viewing the political balance of power as a zero-sum game, "total spoilers" would insist on nothing short of white control.[39] Eventually, Hampton, whose own views would become increasingly stringent, would become their champion. Such an outcome would be unsurprising to John Mearsheimer, who in his analysis of Bosnia argued that "history records no instance where ethnic groups have agreed to share power in a democracy after a large-scale civil war."[40]

In his study of democratization, Samuel Huntington would place the Port Royal Experiment and the Reconstruction era within the "first wave" which began in the 1820s and continued for almost a century. He attributes this wave to such factors as greater economic opportunities, the weakness of existing status systems, and the impact of the Enlightenment, and this analysis is consistent with the positive political developments on the Sea Islands. However, Huntington also notes a reversal or transition away from democracy at the end of this wave that resulted from such factors as the weakness of democratic values among key elite groups, social and political polarization, the determination of conservative middle- and upper-class groups to exclude lower-class groups from political power, and the breakdown of law and order.[41] These factors are also present in the reversal of democratization engineered by white conservatives in South Carolina.

This white opposition was facilitated by the country's growing weariness with Reconstruction, and the contested presidential election of 1877 served as the catalyst for ending the federal military presence in the South. The withdrawal of federal troops from the South Carolina statehouse ended the standoff in the gubernatorial election between Hampton and Republican incumbent Daniel Chamberlain and allowed Hampton to peacefully assume office. Hampton then proceeded to solidify Home Rule and Redemption, supporting Huntington's assertion that transitions away from democracy often occur when a democratically elected chief executive effectively ends democracy by concentrating power in his own hands. These developments will be more fully addressed in chapter 9, "Spoiler Problems and Resistance."

Delaying this discussion, the question for the present is what does the Port Royal Experiment suggest about the ability of military intervention to build liberal democracy. Such an enterprise certainly has a checkered history, with most scholars doubtful of the prospects. The fundamental causes of democracy, they argue, are internal, and most relatively poor, inequitable, and divided societies with illiberal cultural values such as antebellum South Carolina contain impediments to democratization that external intervention will rarely overcome.[42] According to Jeffrey Pickering and Mark Peceny, governments characteristically intervene initially in the interest of national security and only as an afterthought begin to think of also spreading democracy.[43] This was certainly the case at the strategic level in the Civil War, with the federal objective initially being to restore the Union and only later coming to embrace emancipation as well. The same is true at the operational level with the military expedition to Port Royal being launched as a means of strengthening the blockade; only after its success did authorities begin to address the contraband situation. The negative consequences of not deliberately planning the democratization aspect of a military intervention would seem to be intuitive.

Pickering and Peceny suggest that "hostile U.S. interventions" generate initial gains in political liberalization that may persist but do not increase.[44] In gross terms, such was the experience at Port Royal. The slaves were emancipated by the war, and they remained free in its aftermath. Their fledgling right to vote and hold office was secure for a period that roughly coincided with the federal military occupation, but after 1877, for all practical purposes, control of South Carolina's political destiny was restored to its white population. Beyond the temporary franchise, the black population in South Carolina did not experience sustained increases in democratization until well into the twentieth century. In fact, before that day would come, they would endure the loss of many of the political gains that the military intervention and its accompanying Port Royal Experiment had initially delivered.

CHAPTER NINE

Spoiler Problems and Resistance

The Port Royal Experiment and the overall effort to transition former slaves on the South Carolina Sea Islands to freedom during and after the American Civil War illustrate the challenges to peace Stephen Stedman argues arise from "spoiler" position, number, and type as well as the locus of the spoiler problem.[1] Stedman defines spoilers as "leaders and parties who believe the peace emerging from negotiations threatens their power, worldview, and interests."[2] He advises that "custodians of peace" must develop and implement effective strategies to manage spoilers. Edward Pierce, Rufus Saxton, and Oliver Howard, three of the chief custodians of the peace at Port Royal, were besieged by attacks from spoilers that bore Stedman's characteristics. The position of the spoilers ranged from Army officers who were inside the peace process to former Confederates who were outside of it. The existence of a large number of spoilers was demonstrated by the machinations associated with the sale of lands confiscated by the U.S. government. There were also various types of spoilers, including limited ones such as refugee whites with legitimate survival needs; greedy ones such as unscrupulous cotton agents; and total ones such as those who wanted to restore white political, social, and economic domination. Because the white population initially abandoned the Sea Islands, the locus of the problem changed as new spoiler leadership returned after the war was over. These challenges were exacerbated by the Port Royal Experiment's own organizational inefficiencies, many of which are representative of what Stedman calls the "fog of peacemaking."[3]

Gerald Kraus ascribes nation builders who focus on the problem of spoilers as being part of the "liberal imperialism" school.

Adherents, Kraus argues, stress "the need to give an international mission sufficient authority to overcome the efforts of those who seek to obstruct postconflict peacebuilding."[4] According to this theory, "It is only when a peace-building mission is given unlimited powers and significant resources, and only when it is prepared to stay the course for an unlimited period of time, that society can be transformed and a viable state be built."[5] Liberal imperialism's advocates champion the "Brcko model" from Bosnia, recommending that "would-be nation-builders . . . install a powerful interim administrator who is unafraid of defying the local political bosses."[6] The Port Royal Experiment not only confirms Stedman's analysis of spoiler behavior; it also serves as an instructive case study of a nation building and development effort as viewed through the lens of the liberal imperialism school.

"Custodians of Peace"

Stedman defines custodians of the peace as those "actors whose task is to oversee the implementation of peace agreements."[7] Custodians have a variety of spoiler management strategies from which to choose, and Stedman considers the role played by these actors to be "the crucial difference between the success and failure of spoilers."[8] Edward Pierce, Rufus Saxton, and Oliver Howard represent the key custodians of the peace during various stages of the Port Royal Experiment. All three quickly encountered a range of spoilers.

Edward Pierce was a Boston attorney who Secretary of the Treasury Salmon Chase dispatched to Port Royal to investigate the unfolding situation and recommend a plan. Pierce left New York for Port Royal on January 13, and on February 3 he submitted a report to Chase that ultimately would become the blueprint for the Port Royal Experiment.

In his report, Pierce identified several potential spoilers—all of whom would be internal to the peace process. The biggest threat he foresaw was the one arising from conflict of interest. "No man," he wrote, "not even the best of men, charged with the duties which ought to belong to the guardians of these people, should be put in a position where there would be such a conflict between his humanity and self-interest—his desire, on the one hand, to benefit the laborer, and, on the other, the too often stronger desire to reap a large revenue—perhaps to restore fortunes broken in a year or two."[9] Potential for such abuse was represented by Lieutenant Colonel William Reynolds who had arrived in Beaufort on December 20 under Chase's authority to collect contraband cotton. "Time would prove" that this spoiler would not be able to "withstand tempting opportunities to coin money from the war effort."[10]

Pierce also advised Chase of "another precaution most necessary to be taken." In Pierce's mind, "as much as possible, persons enlisted in the army and navy should be kept separate from these people."[11] Indeed, Gideonite Laura Towne would later complain of a regiment of New York soldiers who were "doing all sorts of mischief," including threatening Sea Islanders and stealing their property.[12] The very people tasked with protecting the population at times acted as spoilers.

Another key custodian was Brigadier General Rufus Saxton, a Massachusetts native who graduated from West Point in 1849. His original assignment at Port Royal was as chief quartermaster, and in that capacity he earned the reputation as "the only officer much interested in the work for the contrabands."[13] His role expanded exponentially on April 29, 1862, when he was ordered by Secretary of War Edwin Stanton to "take possession of all the plantations heretofore occupied by rebels, and take charge of the inhabitants remaining thereon within the department, or which the fortunes of war may hereafter bring into it." Saxton reported only to the War Department and Department of the South commander Major General David Hunter, and Stanton empowered Saxton to make "such rules and regulations for the cultivation of the land, and for the protection, employment and government of the inhabitants as circumstances may require."[14] Such an undertaking was unprecedented, and historian Willie Lee Rose declares that "upon [Saxton's] slight shoulders would fall the total responsibility for the agglomeration of people, ideas, and conflicting interests at Port Royal."[15] His service continued with the end of the war when he became the assistant commissioner for the states of South Carolina, Georgia, and Florida of the newly created Freedmen's Bureau.

In spite of his own strong belief in land distribution as the surest guarantee of freedom and conduit to full citizenship, Saxton found himself besieged by spoilers, many of whom were inside the peace process.[16] Rose, for example, describes Saxton as "stranded amid unsympathetic or openly-hostile fellow-officers."[17] He was particularly vexed by Hunter's second-in-command, Brigadier General John Brannan, and he received little help among his own staff save for Captain Edward Hooper, whom Towne considered "the best fellow who ever lived."[18] "My authority," Saxton complained, "has been questioned by the department commanders, explanations of my official acts have been demanded, those acts annulled, and subordinate officers sustained, and encouraged in preventing the execution of my orders."[19] Saxton was so frustrated by internal spoilers he tendered his resignation, only to later withdraw it. Still, the residual tension led to him ultimately being replaced in January 1866 by Brigadier General Robert Scott, a man who unlike Saxton lacked "an unwavering commitment to black rights."[20]

As commissioner of the Freedmen's Bureau, Major General Oliver Howard was custodian of the peace not just on the South Carolina Sea Islands, but throughout the former Confederacy. Biographer William McFeely notes Howard was uniquely qualified for this post because of his Christianity, concern for the freedmen's welfare, freedom from previous entanglements with the work, and outstanding war record.[21] Yet even a man of Howard's stature encountered spoilers, many from within the peace process. The most powerful was President Andrew Johnson, who upon assuming office after the assassination of Abraham Lincoln, embarked on a policy of Reconstruction so magnanimous to white Southerners that it often conflicted with Howard's mandate on behalf of the freedmen. Howard also faced spoilers within his own organization, where action was largely dependent on the world views of the individual agents operating at the local level. Among these were "a sizable group of 'conservatives' [who] often supported coercive labor law with few restrictions and with little commitment to elements of free-labor ideology that promoted social mobility."[22] Of perhaps even greater significance, Howard's efforts were hamstrung by the flawed nature of the Freedmen's Bureau itself, an organization Ezra Warner describes as "riddled by fraud, corruption, and inefficiency, which Howard's religious zeal, personal honesty, and lack of administrative ability was helpless to combat."[23]

Pierce, Saxton, and Howard were joined by countless other laborers as custodians of the peace on the Sea Islands. These three are illustrative because they represent men who operated with a mandate and an accompanying degree of authority yet were still plagued by spoilers, even from within their own ranks. In spite of their personal skill and commitment to the task, they found many challenges to their roles as custodians.

Position of the Spoilers

Stedman notes that "spoilers can be inside or outside a peace process."[24] Those outside the process are willing to use overt violence to undermine the peace while those operating on the inside use stealth to manipulate the peace process to their advantage.[25] The custodians of the peace at Port Royal faced both inside and outside spoilers.

Part of the problem of inside spoilers resulted from the poor planning that plagued the Port Royal Experiment from its inception. The division of labor and authority between Pierce and Reynolds is one example. Reynolds had been empowered to confiscate not just cotton, but everything "movable," and by the time Pierce arrived, he found little left of the common household items he needed to establish his operation. Pierce's protests to Reynolds fell on deaf ears, and the two men reached an impasse. The root problem was that both men were able to frustrate the work of the other. In order to do his job, Pierce needed the furniture, livestock, and farm equipment Reynolds controlled, and in order to do his job, Reynolds needed the labor that Pierce controlled.[26] While at the moment both men would consider the other a spoiler, time would reveal Reynolds as the true culprit.

In the meantime, Reynolds practiced the stealth techniques Stedman describes as characteristic of inside spoilers. In this respect, Reynolds was so successful that in his initial report to Chase, Pierce declared Reynolds, "notwithstanding many difficulties in his way, has fulfilled his duties with singular fidelity and success."[27] Yet without directly confronting Pierce, Reynolds soon had his agents remove furniture from buildings he knew Pierce was preparing to occupy. He delayed in responding to complaints Pierce made, and he wrote critical letters to Chase, their erstwhile mutual superior, about Pierce and the qualifications of his missionaries.[28] It was not until May 7, 1862, when Colonel William Nobles, one of Reynolds's more abusive agents, physically assaulted Pierce that the tide began to turn decidedly in Pierce's favor with Chase.[29] Inside spoilers, Stedman argues, "need to comply enough to convince others of their goodwill" and therefore "have an incentive to keep their threat hidden."[30] Nobles's violation of this caution brought his spoiler status out in the open, and he was recalled north.[31] Reynolds's true colors soon became apparent as well when he was found promoting an illegal private trade in guns and cotton with Confederate agents.[32] Inside spoilers like Nobles and Reynolds require a veil of legitimacy to succeed, and when they lose that cover they can be more efficiently dealt with by the custodians of peace. Until that development, however, Reynolds and his self-serving operators acted as spoilers against much of Pierce's work.

Another significant segment of inside spoilers were the Freedmen's Bureau agents. In such a widely dispersed and decentralized organization, "field agents could undermine directives from headquarters," a situation exacerbated in South Carolina by the fact that neither Saxton nor Scott took a coordinated approach to labor law as was done elsewhere. Thus, James Schmidt concludes, "the influence of Freedmen's Bureau agents in setting the terms of freedom through labor regulations was crucial."[33] While most took a moderate stance, the conservative agents "operated from open or thinly veiled racial predilections, and they showed little restraint on their use of the military's power to ensure plantation labor and uphold plantation discipline."[34]

Outside spoilers do not operate under the same constraints as inside ones. According to Stedman, they "use overt violence as a strategy toward undermining peace."[35] The starkest example of these spoilers was the Ku Klux Klan, which appeared in South Carolina in 1868 and quickly demonstrated a willingness to use "all weapons at the whites' disposal with ... cold-blooded determination."[36] Richard Zuczek argues the Klan in South Carolina was the logical successor to the antebellum slave patrols, and like the patrols, it "was a mounted, armed symbol of white authority that held unquestioned power of life or death in racial matters."[37] It became "a military force serving the interests of the Democratic party, the planter class, and all those who desired the restoration of white supremacy."[38] As a violent outside spoiler, the Klan advocated total objectives, including the political purpose "to reverse the interlocking changes sweeping over the South during Reconstruction: to destroy the Republican party's infrastructure, undermine the Reconstruction state, reestablish control of the black labor force, and restore racial subordination in every aspect of Southern life."[39]

When Klan violence in South Carolina attracted a massive federal crackdown, its members merely reorganized as "rifle clubs" and resumed the pursuit of their previous purposes while being careful to sufficiently manage conflict so as not to draw more federal troops to the state.[40] These clubs became known commonly as "the red-shirts" after the dyed red flannel shirts they adopted as their uniforms. They were well-armed; experienced in military tactics; and were educated, most having written constitutions. Much of the leadership had served during the Civil War with Lieutenant General Wade Hampton. Now, administrative control rested with Brigadier General James Conner, while Colonel Samuel Pickens commanded an "upper" division and Major Theodore Barker a "lower" one.[41] Initially, Barker was forced to exercise restraint in the low country, where the large majority black population was able to successfully resist white violence.[42] With Hampton's ascendency to the governor's mansion, the rifle clubs expanded their area of operations to include what for the black population had once been the "Sea Island sanctuary of Beaufort County."[43]

Number of Spoilers

Stedman notes that "the presence of more than one spoiler creates a compound challenge for custodians [because] any strategy a custodian chooses to deal with one spoiler has implications for the strategy selected to deal with other spoilers."[44] This phenomenon abounded on the Sea Islands, but the large number of spoilers associated with the sale of lands confiscated by the U.S. government is perhaps the starkest example. In this case, the conflicting agendas and confusion created by the sheer volume of spoilers resulted in an end run around the intentions of the custodians.

Proponents of black land ownership would consider Edward Philbrick a spoiler. When the first land sale was held in February 1863, the Bostonian investor ended up in control of eight thousand acres. Hoping to safeguard at least some of the land from such purchases by northern speculators, Saxton had succeeded in convincing Congress to set aside a portion for military and charitable uses and postpone the sale of the remaining lands until March. Under these revised procedures, black Sea Islanders were able to purchase some two thousand acres, a figure dwarfed by Philbrick's acquisition.[45]

Saxton's policy of preemption hoped to stave off such spoilers when the second sale of forty thousand acres was scheduled for the fall. Again the results were disappointing to proponents of black land ownership. By the end of January 1864, blacks had claimed just six thousand acres, in part because of a process William Gannett declared to be "awkward, incomplete, [and] bungling."[46] In addition to the convoluted procedure, another obstacle in the way of increased participation were conservative tax commissioners William Brisbane and William Wording, who "resisted their government orders" and acted as spoilers in refusing some applications and creating a time-consuming process that discouraged others.[47]

More broadly, the entire notion of preemption and its philosophical implications for the accommodation and assimilation of freedmen into society split even the Gideonites into pro-preemption, anti-preemption, and middle ground camps.[48] With confusion and controversy abounding, Secretary of the Treasury Salmon Chase reversed the preemption policy and announced in mid-February 1864 that black Sea Islanders would in fact have to bid against other buyers.[49] Under these new rules, when the sale was conducted on February 18, most tracts were sold to northern whites for more than eleven dollars per acre.[50] Regarding this class of spoiler, Laura Towne ultimately would decide "there is no hater of the negro like these speculating planters."[51]

Major General William Sherman's Special Field Order No. 15 offered another opportunity, but the delayed federal occupation of what became known as Sherman's reserve acted as another spoiler. Until the early summer of 1865, armed Confederate bands as well as destitute white citizens, seeking only to survive, challenged, often violently, the freedmen for the scant resources available. The arrival of federal troops stemmed some of this havoc but also served to enforce a labor ideology that worked against black land ownership.[52]

It seems odd to consider the president of the United States a spoiler, but for custodians like Saxton and Howard attempting to implement Field Order No. 15, Andrew Johnson filled such a role. Johnson was eager to rebuild the nation peacefully, and on May 29, 1865, he issued an Amnesty Proclamation that allowed former Confederates to be pardoned and have their confiscated lands returned to them. For those who saw the Civil War as a new beginning for black opportunity and equality, Johnson was a spoiler. Indeed, McFeely describes the Amnesty Proclamation as an effort "to balance the books again on prewar lines, not by restoring slavery but by dropping the Negro—the new entry—from national calculations."[53] It was with a heavy heart that on September 12, Howard issued as Bureau Circular 15 a letter drafted by Johnson that ordered confiscated lands restored to their pardoned white owners.[54]

As broad as Circular 15 was, however, it did not apply to the lands that fell under Sherman's Field Order No. 15. With nearly all land on the Sea Islands in some state of legal process, Howard worked feverishly to distribute as much real estate as possible before Johnson's policy crystallized. Saxton forwarded each application for restoration with a standard endorsement explaining, "The freedmen [on these islands] were promised protection of the government in their possession. This order was issued under a great military necessity with the approval of the War Dept. . . . I cannot break faith with them by recommending the restoration of any of these lands."[55] Howard agreed, for the time being at least refusing all applications for restoration of property within the confines of Sherman's reserve. Still, he and Saxton knew their predicament. As Rose explains, "They were caught squarely between the President's orders and their own commitment under the Freedmen's Bureau Act to carry out the resettlement program on the coastal islands."[56]

Howard's hand was forced on September 23 when a number of Edisto Island residents petitioned Johnson directly for their lands. Stedman notes that one impact of having a number of spoilers is that it can create something of a zero-sum game.[57] Indeed, the Edisto whites appealed to Johnson that unless these lands were restored, they had nowhere else to go. Johnson told Howard to go to Edisto and meet with all parties to "endeavor to effect an arrangement mutually satisfactory to freedmen and landowners." In spite of this language, the general clearly understood Johnson's intention was that the dispute by resolved in favor of the whites.[58]

Howard made a desperate attempt at compromise by forming a committee made up of three representatives each from the freedmen, the Freedmen's Bureau, and the planters, but by this point, placating everyone was impossible.[59] By late February and early March, U.S. Army units were forcibly returning lands to their former owners and making freedmen sign labor contracts or leave. Furthermore, Saxton became a casualty of his steadfast support for the freedmen and was replaced by Scott, who was less objectionable to many of the spoilers.[60]

When it came to fulfilling what they understood as their mandate to provide freedmen with land, the custodians of the peace on the Sea Islands simply had too many spoilers with which to contend. Far from simply a matter involving the original white owners and the perspective new black owners, the custodians were bombarded by spoilers ranging from speculators to the new president of the United States. Such a sheer number of spoilers created what Stedman describes as a "fog of peacemaking" against which the custodians lacked the agility and power to contend.[61]

Locus of the Problem

Stedman points to the effect leadership changes can have on the spoiler problem. Before the outcome of the Civil War was decided, the Port Royal Experiment was allowed to proceed in relative isolation "without the presence of the masters."[62] This condition changed with the ultimate Federal victory that William McFeely notes "ironically liberated the white planters who would soon compete for the lands held by the freedmen."[63]

The plight of the white returnees was sufficient to elicit significant sympathy from many Gideonites, and there was a natural tendency among some to identify more with the southern whites than with the former slaves.[64] In fact, the American Union Commission (AUC) had been organized in mid-1864 as a relief agency focused primarily on white refugees. This movement gained strength on January 31, 1866, when the American Freedmen's Aid Commission and the AUC united to form the American Freedmen's Union Commission (AUFC).[65] The AFUC was intended to be a biracial organization that James Miller McKim claimed would ignore "all distinctions of race or color."[66] Even the "Freedmen's Bureau," as reflected in its full title of the "Bureau of Refugees, Freedmen, and Abandoned Lands," was mandated to address the needs of white refugees, and Martin Abbott contends many white South Carolinians, while strongly objecting to the Bureau as an institution, found merit and common cause with individual agents.[67]

What Abbott concludes white South Carolinians found threatening in the Bureau was "that its work would endanger white supremacy."[68] Total spoilers, who Stedman claims "pursue total power and exclusive recognition of authority and hold immutable preferences," mobilized to counter this threat.[69] However, it took time for these total spoilers to become strong enough to act. Kelly Greenhill and Solomon Major, in their response to Stedman, predict such a condition, arguing that a "capabilities-based

model" corrects Stedman's underestimation of "the considerable
influence that structural factors continue to exert on the trajectory of the implementation of the peace process."[70] They contend
that in order to succeed, custodians need not focus unduly on the
type of spoiler, but rather on maintaining a capability and willingness to wield superior power.[71] Certainly, their claim that "it is
the prevailing opportunity structure, not actors' intentions, that
presents them with the available options" appears to be borne out
in the Sea Islands' experience.[72]

Radical Reconstruction initially thwarted the political aspirations of conservative white South Carolinians, but by 1870,
corruption in the Republican Party had "created an opening,
a chance to secure a foothold in the government as a stepping
stone to full control."[73] A Union Reform Party was formed to
challenge Republican power, and wealthy antebellum planter and
Confederate cavalry hero Wade Hampton would soon emerge as
"the leading Lost Cause figure in [South Carolina]—the symbol
of white suffering, for southern honor, and for vindication."[74]
Reflecting Greenhill and Major's assertion that actors "adjust
their goals (but not their preferences) according to the prevailing opportunity structure," Hampton in 1869 wrote fellow Union
Reformer James Connor, "We must by steady, patient, and per-
severing work, get possession of the State Government."[75] Such
conditions did not yet exist in 1870, and the Union Reform Party
suffered a series of statewide defeats, including in the gubernatorial race.

Things were different in 1876, when initial returns gave Hampton, running as a Democrat, a victory in "one of the bloodiest
electoral campaigns in American history."[76] However, the results
were contested as supporters of Hampton's opponent, Republican incumbent Daniel Chamberlain, accused the Democrats of
fraud. For five months, both men claimed to be governor, and
two rival assemblies also claimed to be the legal state house of
representatives. South Carolinian whites, however, were in no
mood to let slip from their grasp "a victory years in the making."[77] That they were able to secure the prize indicates that
a change had occurred in what Greenhill and Major assess as
"the most significant determinant in a peace initiative's ultimate

success." By 1875 in South Carolina, "the distribution of power among the competing factions on the ground and those implementing the peace" had shifted in favor of the conservatives.[78] According to Zuczek, this change occurred because Hampton's backers controlled not just "the all-too-real threat of force" represented by the Red Shirts, but also capital and property. When Hampton declared a "Starve Them Out" policy by which taxes could only be collected by men he had appointed, white South Carolinians responded with enthusiasm. Zuczek concludes that "without the power of compulsion, which the Republicans did not have, neither court rulings nor legislative acts could bring in white money."[79] Even President Ulysses Grant acknowledged the reality, saying "the whole army of the United States would be inadequate to enforce the authority of Governor Chamberlain. The people of that State resolved not to resort to violence, but adopted a mode of procedure much more formidable and effective than any armed demonstration. Unless Governor Chamberlain can compel the collection of taxes, it will be utterly useless for him to expect to maintain authority for any length of time."[80]

Electoral confusion reigned at the national level as well, where Democratic candidate Samuel Tilden defeated Rutherford Hayes in the popular vote, but the electoral count was in dispute over alleged voter fraud in Louisiana, Florida, and South Carolina. Following secretive deliberations and negotiations, a special commission declared Hayes to be president. It is impossible to determine the details, but many observers conclude the decision involved some Bargain of 1877 by which Hayes, in exchange for securing the White House, would grant home rule to the South. Indeed, within two months of assuming office, Hayes ordered the federal troops surrounding the South Carolina statehouse to withdraw, and Hampton peacefully assumed office. By his actions, Hayes sent the clear message that the federal troops would no longer play a role in the political affairs of South Carolina and the rest of the former Confederate states. It was the final triumph of Redemption and the failure of Greenhill and Major's requirement that "if peace accords are to be sustained, the opportunity structure that prevailed during the negotiations must be perpetuated."[81]

The change was soon felt throughout the state. Between 1868 and 1871, before its terror campaign was checked by federal authorities, the Klan was most active in the upstate counties of York, Spartanburg, and Union. In contrast, fear of inciting the large black majority to violence had served to check on white aggression in the low country.[82] Even as late as 1876, Hampton had faced an openly hostile black crowd while delivering a political speech in Beaufort. Journalist Alfred Williams, who accompanied Hampton, described it as "the one failure of the campaign" and could barely conceal his relief as the party withdrew from the place they had "been made to feel hatred every minute and at every step."[83] In the closing days of the 1878 political campaign, however, black political icon Robert Smalls was surrounded at Gillisonville, just outside of his Beaufort County base, by "eight hundred red-shirt men, led by colonels, generals, and many leading men of the state."[84] In the subsequent election that year, the balance of power had shifted so decisively that Red Shirt units parading past polling places were able to intimidate enough Republican voters to hand Smalls his first defeat in what had previously been a "black paradise."[85]

Types of Spoilers

Stedman categorizes spoilers as "limited, greedy, and total" and considers identification of goals and commitments as "the first step toward successful management of spoiler problems."[86] The custodians of the peace at Port Royal had to contend with Stedman's entire gamut of spoilers, a task compounded by the changing locus of the problem. Ultimately, the total spoilers succeeded in thwarting the efforts of the custodians and rolling back many of the freedmen's gains.

Among the most limited spoilers were those white returnees who had lost so much of their former way of life that they manipulated or accepted charity from the freedmen to survive. William Elliott, for example, found his family's Oak Lawn manor burned and in ruins, and he was reduced to living in an outhouse with his father's former slaves.[87] Laura Towne reported that when

Gabriel Capus returned, "he went to his people, told him he had no money and nothing to eat, and begged them to let him stay with him. Old Rina took him in, and he lives in her house."[88] Likewise, compassionate freedmen took pity on an impoverished Dr. Clarence Fripp and collected nearly one hundred dollars to help sustain him.[89] So long as the returning whites were weak and few in number, the blacks were able to extend them small kindnesses, but they resisted white efforts to restore the old order.[90]

But few of even these downtrodden white returnees intended on being limited spoilers for long. T. Edwin Ruggles noted this phenomenon in a May 6, 1865, letter that reported, "Secesh are coming back quite freely nowadays and looking about as much as they please."[91] Towne complained that in spite of Rina's kindness, Capus "begins already to show airs" and had warned the freedmen "to buy no more land, as he shall soon have possession of it again."[92] By September, Towne was complaining, "'Secesh' are coming back thick. . . . They are crawlingly civil as yet, but will soon feel their oats."[93] For the time being, the odds were against the native whites of Port Royal, but few were willing to accept their new circumstances as the final outcome.

Before the locus of the spoiler problem changed sufficiently for the native whites to mount a threat as total spoilers, the custodians of the peace had to contend with greedy spoilers from within the peace process. Rose describes the Port Royal Experiment in part as an ambiguous "philanthropic-commercial venture" that attracted many "planter-missionaries [that] were pure economic imperialists."[94] McFeely identifies "northern predators" as the "subtle enemy" that posed "the real threat" to Saxton's efforts on behalf of the freedmen.[95] Even Gideonites such as Edward Philbrick seem to have succumbed to the "conflict between [a man's] humanity and self-interest" about which Pierce originally cautioned.[96] In the first land sale of March 9, 1863, exactly one year after the arrival of the Gideonites, Philbrick purchased eleven cotton plantations, totaling eight thousand acres, and leased two others from the government on behalf of a Boston consortium. For just seven thousand dollars, Philbrick gained control of one-third of the sea island of St. Helena.[97] Many, including Towne, suspected Philbrick of profiteering, and even Philbrick acknowledged the temptation, confessing "it may be difficult to fathom one's own motives in such cases."[98] From the point of view of the freedmen, however, Rose believes the issue was much clearer. For them, Philbrick was "the embodiment of a man whose good motives had been corrupted by good fortune."[99] He was among the "pompous men who had the folly to identify their own economic advantage with the truest philanthropy."[100] To be sure, there were unashamed greedy spoilers that descended on Port Royal like vultures only to exploit and manipulate for personal gain, but the case of Philbrick shows that custodians of the peace must be aware of more subtle situations as well.

Without a doubt, however, the change in the locus of the spoiler problem wrought by the return of the native white population and its resistance to Reconstruction represented the greatest threat. These total spoilers demanded nothing less than the restoration of white political, social, and economic domination. When the violent activities of the Ku Klux Klan between 1868 and 1871 led to federal intervention, the spoilers realized they were "no match for a United States Government that would take seriously its duty to enforce the post–Civil War amendments." They also learned, however, that this threat of federal intervention was "the one obstacle that had to be overcome," and when it was, "the way would be open for the restoration of political rule based on white supremacy." To be sure, the Red Shirts were instrumental in bringing Hampton to power in 1876, but they did so only with "the acquiescence of a passive Federal government."[101]

Organizational Inefficiencies

In combating spoilers, custodians of the peace are not immune from their own limitations, many of which are organizational.[102] The eclectic and ad hoc nature of the Gideonites as a first response to the situation on the Sea Islands makes organizational analysis problematic. The Freedmen's Bureau, however, was designed specifically by the U.S. government as a deliberate and official custodian of the peace. Nonetheless, it was unable to deal effectively with the spoilers it encountered, in large part because it had been created with "insufficient means for doing the work expected of it."[103]

Chief among the Bureau's problems were scarce resources, especially in terms of money and personnel. In creating the Bureau, Congress allocated no funds for its use, instead believing the Bureau could generate its own income from the sale and rental of abandoned and confiscated land, including some three hundred thousand acres on the Sea Islands, as well as the sale of cotton there. Instead, the proceeds from the cotton, some three hundred thousand dollars worth, went to Secretary Chase's Treasury Department instead of the Bureau, and by President Johnson's order of September 1865, the land was largely returned to its former owners. As a result, by 1866 the Bureau's rental income had dropped to fifty dollars a month from the six thousand dollars a month it had collected a year earlier. Abbott notes "the inevitable result was a sharp curtailment in [the Bureau's] program at a time when the need for its assistance among the people was greatest."[104]

Personnel shortages also hamstrung the Bureau's effectiveness in South Carolina to the degree "that it could never adequately serve the needs demanded by its responsibilities."[105] In the Colleton district, for example, one officer and one agent were responsible for the affairs of forty thousand freedmen.[106] In Beaufort, Agent H. G. Judd reported seventeen thousand freedmen had arrived between January and August 1865.[107] Help to the Bureau would not be forthcoming as departmental commander Major General Quincy Gillmore made clear the priorities, informing Saxton in October, "the interests of the service will not permit the detailing of officers from their regiments."[108]

At its peak strength in mid-1867, the Bureau in South Carolina boasted a total force of just eighty-eight, of whom only forty were agents or officers in the field.[109] The result, according to Randall Miller, was "the caseload of individual agents was staggering."[110] For a man of modest talent like Judd, who Rose considers to have been "apparently honest" yet who "managed badly," the difficulties would be compounded.[111]

This personnel shortage was exacerbated by the fact that the military officers assigned as agents were responsible to both the

Bureau's assistant commissioner and the departmental military commander, and their loyalties tended to remain with the military hierarchy. In the Beaufort area, the military commander refused to convene a board more than once a month to examine all applications for relief. Although widespread suffering was reported among those unable to appear before the board, the protests of the local Bureau agent were disregarded by military authorities. Such dependency on the whims of the military hierarchy led Scott to complain that he "was merely the medium for the transmittal of orders."[112] Saxton was even more vexed, claiming the Army treated Bureau agents as if they were "enemies of the United States Government."[113]

On June 30, 1872, the Bureau was formally disbanded, and its unfinished business was transferred to the office of the assistant adjutant general of the Army.[114] Perhaps here was the Bureau's most serious organizational flaw. Although always intended to be an agent of transition, the Bureau, and with it the Port Royal Experiment, lacked the perseverance necessary to give that transition the traction it needed. Once the spoilers realized the temporary nature of the custodians of peace on the Sea Islands, they acted accordingly.[115] Giving credit to the successful strategy of these spoilers, Zuczek concludes that "in the end, Reconstruction did not fail; it was defeated."[116]

Spoiler Victory

Stedman identifies three major strategies to manage spoilers: inducement, socialization, and coercion. He notes custodians "can employ more than one strategy—either simultaneously (with different priority and emphasis) or in sequence," and, indeed, all three were tried on the Sea Islands.[117] Nonetheless, ultimate success was elusive.

Inducement involves "taking positive measures to address the grievances of factions who obstruct peace." In short, it hopes to secure spoiler cooperation by "meeting the spoiler's demands."[118] This strategy is represented by the land sales that catered to speculators. The strategy of socialization requires parties to comply with established norms, and "these norms then become the basis of judging the demands of the parties."[119] President Johnson's Amnesty Proclamation is an example of an attempt at socialization. Coercion "relies on the use or threat of punishment to deter or alter unacceptable spoiler behavior or reduce the capability of the spoiler to disrupt the peace process."[120] The federal crackdown against Klan activity in 1871 successfully employed this strategy.

Following Stedman's argument, the overall failure of these combined strategies is best attributed to the custodians' failure to match the strategy to the type of spoiler.[121] When the white Confederates returned to South Carolina, the change in the locus of the problem made these total spoilers the main threat. Stedman explains that inducement and socialization are inappropriate counters to the total spoiler's "all-or-nothing terms," and instead he recommends a coercive approach.[122] However, because the total spoilers applied Greenhill and Major's prescription of building capabilities until they became able "to unilaterally achieve a better deal than the one on the table," they were in a position to challenge a coercive strategy based on the declining federal willingness to use force.[123] President Grant's description of Chamberlain's impotency to challenge Hampton's claim to the governor's office testifies to this shift in power.

In the end, the custodians withdrew, a strategy Stedman cautions "backfires against a total spoiler, who has everything to gain if custodians abandon the peace process."[124] The only chance a strategy of departure has to succeed is if the custodians first "deprive the spoiler of resources—both capital and weapons."[125] Hampton's tax policy and the Red Shirts certainly demonstrated this condition did not exist.

In the final analysis, it appears the failure to deal appropriately with total spoilers as required by Stedman as well as the failure to maintain the capability and willingness to wield power as required by Greenhill and Major combined to frustrate the custodians of the peace on the Sea Islands. In the post–Cold War era, it became popular to attribute the difficulty of achieving self-sustaining peace in the Balkans, Somalia, Iraq, and elsewhere to

total spoilers willing to wait for the shift in opportunity capability that accompanied the inevitable waning of U.S. interest and
will. Rather than a new phenomenon, this strategy appears to
be one with which America has considerable experience, both as
custodian and spoiler.

CHAPTER TEN

The Hand in the Bucket: Sequencing and Perseverance

Nation building is a complicated and complex subject that invites a variety of opinions and emotions. The controversy begins with the inherent value of the concept itself. On the one hand, David Tucker argues in his highly critical "Facing the Facts: The Failure of Nation Assistance," that the very idea of nation assistance "is a bad one, and should be expunged from policy, doctrine, and practice."[1] On the other, Paul Miller writes in "The Case for Nation-building: Why and How to Fix Failed States" that "nation-building is a necessary response to the danger of failed states that threaten regional stability. . . . It is a pragmatic exercise of hard power to protect vital national interests."[2] Assuming that nation building is a worthwhile pursuit, there are two general schools of thought concerning how it should be practiced. One is the "planning school," epitomized by James Dobbins, which "prescribes a clear strategy, metrics, and structure, backed by overwhelming resources." The second is the "liberal imperialist school" represented by Paddy Ashdown, which "emphasizes the importance of decisive, bold, and charismatic leadership."[3] In some of the most recent scholarship based on experiences in Afghanistan and Bosnia, Rory Stewart and Gerald Knaus reject both these traditional schools in favor of "principled incrementalism/passionate moderation."[4] According to this construct, "intervention . . . is not a scientific method but a practical activity with a humanitarian purpose."[5] It is inherently uncertain and an art rather than a science.[6] Jeremi Suri, another recent scholar of the subject, agrees that "real nation-building is messy and unruly; Americans fail when they try to make it neat and tidy."[7]

But as anyone who has tried to raise children, invest in the stock market, or farm can attest, life is full of activities that involve uncertainty, volatility, and change. This reality does not eliminate the wisdom of planning. It merely requires the flexibility and agility to adjust and change that plan to the situation as it unfolds. Suri captures this notion in asserting that "effective nation-building always proceeds. . . from simplistic doctrine to creative adaptation."[8] The Port Royal Experiment certainly supports this understanding.

Doctrine, even if it is "simplistic," provides some sort of conceptual framework, common vocabulary, basis for prioritization and allocation of resources, and means of measuring progress to an objective. It is a means rather than an end, but it does provide the vehicle through which unity of effort can be achieved. The Port Royal Experiment, with its ad hoc and fragmented approach to policy, planning, and organization, lacked this component.

Chaos theory describes dynamical systems that are deterministic, recurrent, and have sensitive dependence on their initial state.[9] When applied to a nation-building operation like the one at Port Royal that begins with a marked lack of definition, chaos theory suggests the process is not likely to move toward clarity. In fact, the natural course is toward increased uncertainty. The Port Royal Experiment's deficiency in initial planning and policy no doubt contributed to its ensuing difficulties with unity of effort and perseverance.

In the absence of even "simplistic doctrine," as it unfolded, the Port Royal Experiment was forced to place a premium on "creative adaptation." This ability to adjust was most successful at the local level, as epitomized by the educational initiatives that often depended on the personal energies of individuals such as Laura Towne. Such an outcome is consistent with the predictions of the liberal imperialist school of nation building. On the other hand, the Port Royal Experiment found it more difficult to develop, "on the fly," far-reaching solutions to broad, complex problems like land reform at the strategic level. The planning school of nation building would predict as much.

As a result of these inconsistencies, most observers have assessed the Port Royal Experiment as at best a mixed success. Certainly, it succeeded in meeting immediate humanitarian needs and beginning the transition from slavery to freedom for the Sea Islands blacks. However, these early gains reached a plateau, and not only did not become self-sustaining and increasing, but as time passed they regressed. In this regard, the Port Royal Experiment can be likened to placing one's arm in a bucket of water. When the arm is submerged, the water immediately rises and while the arm remains in place, the water level stays elevated but no longer increases. When the arm is removed, however, the water level subsides. The change is wholly dependent on the outside force and has no inherent ability to sustain itself, let alone to generate its own activity. At the very best, when the outside force is removed, there is a return to the original equilibrium.

Such reversals notwithstanding, Jeffrey Pickering and Mark Peceny, in spite of their overall caution, note that "some states have democratized in the wake of military interventions."[10] Developers must then determine why some efforts succeed and others fail. Two main potential explanations are readily apparent. The first is a general lack of perseverance on the part of the developers (the willingness to keep the arm in the bucket for a sufficient length of time). The second is, even if such perseverance is present, there is an inappropriate sequencing of liberalization and institutions (the presence of the necessary capabilities for the fledgling democracy to sustain itself after the arm is withdrawn). Both of these phenomena were present in the negative forms at Port Royal, and both have continued to plague more recent nation-building efforts.

Francis Fukuyama frames the issue by arguing that the nation-building process really consists of three distinct aspects or phases. These are the postconflict reconstruction, the creation of self-sustaining state institutions, and the strengthening of weak states.[11] It is in the first phase that the military plays its most important and specific role.

During the postconflict reconstruction phase, Fukuyama acknowledges the need for outside powers to provide "short-term provision of stability through infusions of security forces, police, humanitarian relief, and technical assistance to restore electricity, water, banking and payment systems, and so on."[12] Obviously, the provision of security and restoration of basic physical life-sustaining infrastructure is within the military's capability, and there should be a specific role for the military to play. Fukuyama's definition of nation building also requires an occupational authority in order to provide the direct leverage that an external position cannot.[13] Obviously, a military presence provides such leverage.

The problem lies in the transition from phase one to phase two. The military must not just establish security; it must be able to transition the ongoing responsibility for maintenance of that security to someone else. An international peacekeeping force, a retrained police force, and a newly formed apolitical and civilian-controlled host-nation military are all candidates to assume the security function, but their realization has in each case been elusive. Building on the "modicum of security" established in phase one, the goal Fukuyama identifies during phase two "is to create self-sustaining state institutions that can survive the withdrawal of outside intervention."[14] However, he warns, if this is what nation building means, "then the number of historical cases where this has happened successfully drops to a depressingly small handful."[15]

Phase three overlaps with phase two and "involves the strengthening of weak states where state authority exists in a reasonably stable form but cannot accomplish certain necessary functions like the protection of property rights or the provision of basic primary education."[16] Fukuyama emphasizes that the "strength of state institutions is more important in a broad sense than the scope of state functions."[17] This is to say that the ability of a state to "plan and execute policies and to enforce laws cleanly and transparently" is more important than "the different functions and goals taken on by governments."[18] The implication is that, although there is "no agreed-on hierarchy of state functions . . . there has to be *some* degree of hierarchy"[19] (emphasis in original). Prioritization of finite resources is necessary, some services are more important than others, and some sequencing is required.

The Port Royal Experiment seemed to unfold in the exact opposite order of the one suggested by Fukuyama. The first group to arrive in force after the Federal victory was the Gideonites in 1862. They brought with them a focus on primary education—the very sort of specific function Fukuyama recommends being reserved for phase three after security and self-sustaining institutions have been established. The next group to arrive was the Freedmen's Bureau—created in 1865 and potentially a good candidate for the transition work required in phase two. However, because there was no foundation laid in phase one and because of the Bureau's own organizational limitations, insufficient self-sustaining growth was established. The final group on the scene was the military, which of course had had some presence from the very beginning but arrived with significant strength and mandate only with the advent of Radical Reconstruction in 1867. The reason Fukuyama places the military in his phase one is its ability to provide security and create order. The military presence during Radical Reconstruction fulfilled this objective, but because insufficient self-sustaining institutions were built along the way, when the military withdrew, the security and order withdrew with it.

Dan Reiter offers a similar analysis of the democratization process by saying it consists of two phases. The first is the transition phase, which involves "the movement from a system of authoritarian rule to one of institutionalized, democratic governance." During this phase, Reiter notes that the former authoritarian leaders must be convinced "to accept a political system that may leave them out of power."[20] This requirement was not accomplished on the Sea Islands, where conservative whites rejected the notion of black political leadership.

Reiter's second phase is the survival phase in which fragile new democracies are especially vulnerable "if those left out of power seek to regain control by destroying these new institutions." This course was the one followed by the conservative whites, and by 1877, they had "redeemed" their state. They then began the systematic process that by 1895 would provide for the outright disfranchisement of most of the black population. To avoid these pitfalls and create a successful transition to democracy, Reiter argues that "the institutionalization and legitimization of democracy" must be ensured.[21]

This idea of the criticality of institutions has received much attention in the wake of the host of democratization efforts the international community launched in the post–Cold War era. Indeed, Fukuyama contends that "institutions matter has been a watchword since at least 1997."[22] For many observers, this importance translates into the need for careful and deliberate sequencing of the democratization process. Roland Paris, for example, insists on the need for "institutionalization before liberalization," or IBL. According to this theory, "peacebuilders should concentrate on constructing a framework of effective institutions prior to promoting political and economic competition." Paris says this process can be accomplished by waiting until conditions are ripe for elections, designing electoral systems that reward moderation, promoting good civil society, controlling hate speech, adopting conflict-reducing economic policies, and rebuilding effective state institutions.[23] On the Sea Islands, few of these prerequisites were accomplished.

Paris insists peacebuilders must postpone elections "until moderate political parties have been created."[24] He believes "the most dangerous circumstances are those in which the principal contenders for election are the very individuals or organizations that recently fought the civil war, particularly if these individuals and groups exploit intercommunal fears and hatreds in order to build electoral support."[25] In the election of April 1868, nearly the entire Republican ticket was elected. Whatever these new officeholders' intentions may have been, the white conservative population viewed them as hostile. As a result they launched a campaign to regain power, which led to a similarly decisive Democratic victory less than a decade later. Paris's theory suggests this whiplash effect could be mitigated by delaying elections until moderate parties who "seem genuinely committed to resolving disputes through peaceful negotiation and to intercommunal reconciliation have sufficient popular support."[26]

In calling for electoral systems that reward moderation, Paris advocates rules that "require candidates to secure a minimum level of support in communities other than their own."[27] Otherwise, there is a danger politicians will come to power "on the basis of their credentials [which on the Sea Islands largely equated to race and party], not as conciliators but as defenders of their own group's interests over and above the interests of their ethnic adversaries."[28] Edward King wrote prophetically in 1875 that black South Carolinians "will learn in time they have committed a grave error in allowing the whites to be virtually excluded from representation, and that both races will be forced to labor together, honestly and faithfully, to save the State, and to insure their own future prosperity."[29] Instead, politics on the Sea Islands largely became a zero-sum game, dominated first by black interests and then by white ones, with little room for moderation and cooperation.

Paris's requirements to promote good civil society and control hate speech were also unfulfilled. The rifle clubs were the best example of the "bad" civil society Paris argues must be restrained. Instead, they became powerful enough to use violence and the threat of violence to undermine democratization. On the other hand, "good" civil society was underdeveloped, leading, for example, John Rachal to bemoan the missed opportunity to advance adult education.[30] The ensuing low level of black literacy made newspapers an imperfect source of the responsible information Paris requires.[31] This connection between two of Paris's key elements reinforces his call for a deliberate, sequential approach.

Paris's charge to adopt conflict-reducing economic policies was also imperfectly addressed on the Sea Islands. On this front, the executors of the Port Royal Experiment were divided on their adherence to market-oriented or state-dominated development strategies. While admitting that "debates continue over the appropriate balance," Paris determines market-oriented policies to be a necessary, although probably not a sufficient, condition for sustained economic growth.[32] However, given the overwhelming obstacles presented to the former slaves, the situation seems to require the "developmental state" approach advocated by Chalmers Johnson that promotes strong state intervention in the private sector in order to guide development in accordance with national interests. Johnson argues that only the government can provide this direction because it is protected from the vagaries of business and labor influences.[33]

The problem on the Sea Islands was that there was no consensus on the national interest at stake and no deliberate governmental economic developmental strategy, either of the type advocated by Johnson or otherwise. Instead, the government itself became the source of the very vagaries Johnson charges it to mitigate, such as the vacillating land policy on the Sea Islands. The result was that development could not unfold in Johnson's "plan-rational" way, because there was no plan. Echoing Paris's emphasis on institutions, Johnson argues such development requires "market-rational political institutions," chiefly the "economic bureaucracy" he considers the "apparatus of plan rationality."[34] Unfortunately, there was little tradition of such a bureaucracy in antebellum Beaufort where there had been neither a local bank nor other financial agency. Instead, cotton factors serviced the planters credit needs between annual harvests.[35] Thus, a void existed when the federal forces arrived on the scene.

There is successful precedent for outside forces filling such a void, with Johnson contending Japan's success in developing its economic bureaucracy was largely the result of reforms generated by its post–World War II Allied occupiers.[36] On the Sea Islands, the congressionally chartered Freedman's Savings Bank and Trust Company was one effort that potentially could have had a similar effect. While the Beaufort branch of this organization was plagued by scandal at the hands of a dishonest cashier, setting this personal failure aside, the bank still did not attempt to fulfill a developmental function after Johnson's model. Rather than investing in local schools, hospitals, or model villages like the one at Mitchelville, the branch issued preferential loans that mostly benefited land speculators, former missionaries, and northern merchants.[37] Thus, what represented a once-promising developmental initiative collapsed in failure in 1874.

All of these arguments emphasize the need for perseverance and long-term commitment, and Paris recognizes that his IBL strategy will require international missions to remain in place longer than they previously have been.[38] Nonetheless, he stresses that "peacebuilders should delay liberalization and limit political and economic reforms in the short run in order to create conditions for a smoother and less hazardous transition to market democracy—and durable peace—in the long run."[39] He is aware that opponents may object to what they may portray as an "endless mission," but counters that the "quick and dirty" approach is "fundamentally flawed" and that the IBL approach is "in the long run" less costly and much more likely to achieve "a stable and lasting peace."[40]

Unfortunately, events on the Sea Islands unfolded with the rush to liberalization without first building institutions against which Paris cautions. Willie Lee Rose criticizes, for example, "the federal government's granting voting rights without providing the means for national assistance to education."[41] Edward Mansfield and Jack Snyder agree that such a sequential approach is essential. "Our most general rule," they explain, "is to start the process by building the institutions that democracy requires, and then encouraging mass political participation and unfettered electoral competition only after these institutions have begun to take root."[42] When elections are held before the prerequisite institutions are in place, "political competition typically coalesces around and reinforces the ethnic and sectarian divisions in traditional society."[43] Certainly, that was the outcome with white and black Sea Islanders. Mansfield and Snyder further caution that "once a country starts on an illiberal trajectory, ideas are unleashed and institutions are established that tend to continue propelling it along that trajectory."[44] The Black Codes, corruption, and Red Shirts certainly can be seen as evidence of this premature democratization on the Sea Islands.

Huntington's solution is to restrict political participation and mobilization during the formative stages of development, if necessary through the temporary establishment of authoritarian military governments. Guardian military rule, he asserts, is often the only viable means of managing the destabilizing effects of change and creating effective political institutions that can, at a later date, be placed under civilian and democratic control.[45] The military, he writes, are "the apostles of order," and in the midst of sea changes such as the one wrought by the Federal victory in the Civil War, order is often what is most required.[46] "Men may, of course, have order without liberty," Huntington notes, "but they cannot have liberty without order." The first requirement for development, then, is "the creation of a legitimate public order."[47]

Many proponents of this military presence base their argument on the idea that state-building in its strictest sense is about creating the Weberian monopoly of violence over a defined territory. Paris considers the restoration of this monopoly to be "a foundation and precondition for all further institution-building efforts." He argues that "a peaceful and limited state presupposes an effective state that can, at a minimum, ensure public security."[48] Rory Stewart suggests that regarding Afghanistan "the international community perhaps assume[d], without ever confessing (like many members of the Afghan cabinet), that an authoritarian military state was a necessary phase in state-formation, or a precondition for rapid economic development."[49] The problem that Huntington points out, however, is that "authority has to exist before it can be limited."[50] A rush to liberalization can undermine this reality.

Fukuyama explains the practical dilemma by claiming that securing the Weberian monopoly requires coercion, force, and building central political authority, while building liberal rule of law and democracy involves limiting the state's central authority to coerce. Legitimate monopolies of violence, he reminds, are especially difficult to establish in societies with significant cleavages such as between the black and white Sea Islanders. Rushing the process simply freezes conflicts that will eventually reemerge and threaten whatever democracy has developed in the meantime.[51] James Fearon and David Laitin agree, noting that in postconflict environments where "the state apparatus [has been rendered] too dysfunctional to provide for domestic security . . . some level of sustained transitional administration" will be necessary lest the former belligerents return to violence.[52] The calculated rise of the Red Shirts and the Redeemers certainly bears out these prophecies, and the analyses suggest that only a longer period of federal occupation and reconstruction would have had a chance of building a legitimate state-controlled monopoly of violence.

The Port Royal Experiment and Reconstruction's subsequent developmental effort simply did not reflect this perseverance. Gideonites became homesick or succumbed to other forces of attrition. Relief agencies shifted emphasis to other areas or declared victory too soon. Philanthropies and charitable organizations suffered from donor fatigue. Military requirements dictated manpower be devoted to other battlefields. Soldiers and their families pressed for demobilization. Spoilers sapped the will of custodians of the peace and made progress unbearably difficult and expensive. The nation as a whole was eager to return to some measure of normalcy, even if the work was incomplete. Besides, Willie Lee Rose asserts, "the North had plainly concluded that in granting the franchise the national obligation to the freedmen had been fulfilled."[53]

Back in 1862, Edward Pierce had written Secretary of the Treasury Salmon Chase to propose "the inauguration of a beneficent system which will settle a great social question."[54] The Port Royal Experiment that followed can be classified perhaps best as an example of Robert Burns's caution about "the best laid schemes of mice and men." Rose reports the contemporary assessment that "just as Beaufort and Port Royal had been ten years before the embodiment of Northern hopes for a renovated South, they had now become symbols of the failure of radical Reconstruction and the final effects of a revolution the nation had disowned."[55] Even the indefatigable Laura Towne bemoaned in 1874, "Sometimes it seems like work thrown away."[56] For Towne, this condition just increased her commitment. "I never before thought it so necessary to be here," she wrote, "and I will not even *think* of going"[57] (emphasis in original). Her perseverance was unfortunately not the norm.

If nothing else, the Port Royal Experiment serves as a reminder of Mansfield and Snyder's call for "humility about the ability of any outsider to re-engineer a country's political institutions,"[58] Thomas Carothers's contention that outsiders can rarely have a huge effect on a society's choice of political trajectory,[59] and Rory Stewart's caution that the international community "knows much less and can do much less than we pretend."[60] Fukuyama agrees that nation building has "an extremely troubled record of success," yet he pragmatically notes that, like it or not, it is a necessary response to "the kinds of security and foreign policy needs the United States faces and will face."[61] The same was true in 1862. Given this reality, perhaps the best advice then is for would-be developers to enter the process with realistic expectations and a healthy respect for the lessons that can be learned from their predecessors at Port Royal and elsewhere.

Notes

Chapter One

1. Willie Lee Rose, *Rehearsal for Reconstruction: The Port Royal Experiment* (New York: Bobbs-Merrill, 1964), 6–9.

2. Theodore Rosengarten, *Tombee: Portrait of a Cotton Planter* (New York: William Morrow, 1986), 50–52.

3. Howard Beale, ed., *The Diary of Edward Bates, 1859–1866* (Washington, DC: Government Printing Office, 1933), 195.

4. Rosengarten, 60; Rose, 124–127; Guion Griffis Johnson, *A Social History of the Sea Islands* (Chapel Hill: University of North Carolina Press, 1930), 50–59.

5. Johnson, 83.

6. Edward Pierce, *The Negroes at Port Royal: Report of E. L. Pierce, Government Agent, to the Hon. Salmon P. Chase, Secretary of the Treasury* (Boston, MA: R. F. Wallcut, 1862), 21–22.

7. Johnson, 83.

8. Ibid., 7–8.

9. Ibid., 6.

10. Edward Pierce, "The Freedmen at Port Royal," *North American Review* 101, no. 208 (July 1865): 2.

11. Kevin Weddle, *Lincoln's Tragic Admiral: The Life of Samuel Francis Du Pont* (Charlottesville: University of Virginia Press, 2005), 111.

12. Ibid., 28.

13. JP 5-0, *Joint Operational Planning* (Washington, DC: Joint Chiefs of Staff, 2006), IV-2.

14. Weddle, 107.

15. Ibid., 109.

16. Shelby Foote, *The Civil War: A Narrative*, vol. 1 (New York: Random House, 1958), 116; Russell Weigley, *The American Way of War* (Bloomington: University of Indiana Press, 1973), 99.

17. Herman Hattaway and Archer Jones, *How the North Won* (Urbana: University of Illinois Press, 1983), 127.

18. H. David Stone, *Vital Rails: The Charleston & Savannah Railroad and the Civil War in South Carolina* (Columbia: University of South Carolina Press, 2008), 36, 67, and 141.

19. Bruce Catton, *This Hallowed Ground* (Garden City, NY: Doubleday, 1956), 85; Foote, vol. 1, 116; Rosengarten, 213; Philip Van Doren Stern, *The Confederate Navy: A Pictorial History* (Garden City, NY: Doubleday, 1962), 54; Bern Anderson, *By Sea and by River: A Naval History of the Civil War* (Westport, CT: Greenwood Press, 1962), 53–54.

20. Catton, *Hallowed*, 85; Anderson, 53.

21. Douglas Southall Freeman, *R. E. Lee*, vol. 1 (New York: Charles Scribners' Sons, 1934), 606; Foote, vol. 1, 116–117; Clifford Dowdey and Louis Manarin, *The Wartime Papers of R. E. Lee* (New York: Bramhall House, 1961), 81.

22. Foote, vol 1, 117; Anderson 54; Weddle 131.

23. Weigley, 99–100; W. Scott Poole, *South Carolina's Civil War: A Narrative History* (Macon, GA: Mercer University Press, 2005), 38–39; Rosengarten, 212; Edward Pollard, *The Lost Cause* (New York: E. B., 1867), 193; Foote, vol. 1, 117.

24. Weddle, 130; Poole, 39; Foote, vol. 1, 117.

25. Foote, vol. 1, 117.

26. Weddle, 132.

27. Virgil Jones, *The Civil War at Sea*, vol. 1 (New York: Holt, Rinehart, Winston, 1961), 275.

28. E. Milby Burton, *The Siege of Charleston, 1861–1865* (Columbia: University of South Carolina Press, 1970), 71.

29. Anderson, 55; Foote, vol. 1, 117–119.

30. Jones, 278.

31. Pollard, 194.

32. Poole, 39; Foote, vol. 1, 119; Peter Chaitin, *The Coastal War* (Alexandria, VA: Time-Life Books, 1984), 20.

33. Anderson, 57.

34. Burton, 72–73.

35. Foote, vol 1, 118–119.

36. Weddle, 140–141; Foote, vol. 1, 119–120; Pollard, 194; Anderson, 57–58; Emory Thomas, *The Confederate Nation* (New York: Harper and Row, 1979), 125.

37. Weigley, 101–102.

38. Freeman, vol. 1, 610; Dowdey and Manarin, 82.

39. Anderson, 59.

40. Ibid., 59; Stone, 70.

41. Van Doren Stern, 54.

42. Anderson, 61.

43. Rosengarten, 219–221.

44. David Goldfield et al., *The American Journey* (Upper Saddle River, NJ: Prentice Hall, 2002), 173.

45. Elaine Brooks, "Massachusetts Anti-Slavery Society," *Journal of Negro History* 30, no. 3 (July 1945): 311–312.

46. Rose, 49.

47. John Blum et al., *The National Experience* (New York: Harcourt, Brace, and Jovanovich, 1993), 260.

48. John Wesley, *The Works of the Reverend John Wesley, A. M.* (New York: J. Emory and B. Waugh, 1831), 337.

49. The Bible, King James Version.

50. Wesley, *Works*, 329.

51. John Wesley, *Thoughts upon Slavery* (London: R. Hawes, 1774), 46–47.

52. Poole, 42–43.

53. Pierce, Negroes, 6.

Chapter Two

1. Rose, 199.

2. Weddle, 107.

3. Kevin Dougherty, *Strangling the Confederacy* (Philadelphia: Casemate, 2010), 196–197.

4. Joint Pub 3-0, *Operations* (Washington, DC: Joint Chiefs of Staff, 2006), III-20.

5. Pierce, "Freedmen," 16; Rose, 63.

6. Rose, 12–15.

7. Ibid., 17–18.

8. James Dobbins et al, *The Beginner's Guide to Nation-Building* (Santa Monica, CA: RAND, 2007), 16.

9. Ibid., 16–17.

10. Ibid., 15.

11. Laura Towne, *Letters and Diary of Laura M. Towne*, ed. Rupert Sargent Holland, 60–61 (Cambridge, MA: Riverside Press, 1912).

12. Dobbins, *Beginner's Guide*, 15.

13. Rose, 177.

14. Ibid., xvii.

15. Ibid., 279.

16. Laura Wood Roper, "Frederick Law Olmsted and the Port Royal Experiment," *Journal of Southern History* 31, no. 3 (August 1965): 272.

17. Ibid., 272–273.

18. Rose, 19.

19. Roper, 274–275.

20. Ibid., 275.

21. Ibid., 284.

22. Ibid., 276.

23. Ibid., 276–277.

24. *Massachusetts Historical Society Proceedings* (2nd series), 18, 363; *American Antiquarian Society Proceedings* (new series), 12, 197–210; "Death of Edward L. Pierce," *New York Times*, September 8, 1897.

25. Chase to Pierce (n.d.), quoted in Rose, 22.

26. Rose, 24–25.

27. Johnson, 160.

28. Rose, 21–22.

29. Pierce, Negroes, 25.

30. Ibid., 28.

31. Rose, 31.

32. Pierce, Negroes, 25; Rose, 33.

33. Rose, 34.

34. Roper, 278.

35. Rose, 336.

36. Roper, 279–280.

37. Pierce, "Freedmen," 16.

38. Rose, 70.

39. Towne, 9.

40. Roper, 281.

41. Ibid., 282–283.

42. Ibid., 283.

43. Ibid., 284.

44. Ibid., 284.

45. Ibid., 283.

46. Rose, 291.

47. Ibid., 180 and 278.

48. Ibid., xvii–xviii.

49. Towne, 135.

50. Rose, 23–24.

51. Towne, 57.

52. Rose, 67.

53. William Pease, "Three Years among the Freedmen: William C. Garnett and the Port Royal Experiment," *Journal of Negro History* 42, no. 2 (April 1957): 102.

54. Towne, 7.

55. Ibid., 59–60 and 71.

56. Ibid., 60.

57. Rose, 143. Cotton agents also took pieces of the highly prized furniture with them when they returned North. See Towne, 66.

58. Rose, 222.

59. Ibïd., 27–28.

60. Ibid., 72.

61. Ibid., 73.

62. David Donald, *Inside Lincoln's Cabinet, The Civil War Diaries of Salmon P. Chase* (New York: Longman's, Green, 1954), 71.

63. Rose, 75.

64. Ibid., 219.

65. Towne, 92; Rose, 180.

66. Towne, 127.

67. Rose, 71.

68. Ibid., 335.

69. Ibid., 220–221.

70. Ibid., 76.

71. Ibid., 219.

72. Ibid., 334.

73. Ibid., 75.

74. Ibid., 335.

75. Ibid., 66.

76. Ibid., 66.

77. Towne, 63.

78. Ibid., 8.

79. Pierce, "Freedmen," 16.

80. Rose, 152. See also Towne, 128, for her praise of "one of our best and truest-hearted men."

81. Rose, 153 and 170.

82. Towne, 88 and 90.

83. Pease, 104.

84. Towne, 91.

85. Rose, 178–179.

86. Ibid., 329.

87. Ibid., 330.

88. Ibid., 338.

89. Ibid., 351.

90. Ibid., 356.

91. Ibid., 375–376.

92. Donald Wright and Timothy Reese, *On Point II: Transition to the New Campaign: The United States Army in Operation Iraqi Freedom, May 2003–January 2005* (Fort Leavenworth, KS: Combat Studies Institute Press, 2008), 72.

93. Dobbins, *Beginner's Guide*, 3.

94. James Dobbins, *America's Role in Nation-Building: From Germany to Iraq* (Santa Monica, CA: RAND, 2003), 113.

95. Ibid., 118.

96. Ibid., 126.

97. Jonathan Dworken, "Restore Hope: Coordinating Relief Operations," *Joint Forces Quarterly* 8 (Summer 1995): 19–20.

98. Kenneth Allard, *Somalia Operations: Lessons Learned* (Fort McNair, Washington, DC: National Defense University Press, 1995), 67.

99. Rory Stewart and Gerald Knaus, *Can Intervention Work?* (New York: W. W. Norton, 2011), 129–141.

100. Ibid., 138.

101. Ibid., 188.

102. Ibid., 188.

103. *Oxford English Dictionary*, Online version, March 2012, http://www.oed.com/view/Entry/153584?redirectedFrom=prudence#eid.

Chapter Three

1. Pierce to Chase, January 19, 1862, item 36, Port Royal Correspondence, National Archives, Washington, DC.

2. *The War of the Rebellion: A Compilation of the Official Records of the Union and Confederate Armies*, Series 1, vol. 6 (Washington, DC: Government Printing Office, 1880-1901), 222–223. Hereafter OR.

3. Roper, 279.

4. P. J. Simmons, "Learning to Live with NGOs," *Foreign Policy* 112 (Fall 1998): 87.

5. Rose, 336.

6. Ibid., 30.

7. Pierce to the Reverend Mr. Jacob Manning, January 19, 1862, Edward Atkinson MSS, Massachusetts Historical Society, Boston, MA.

8. Rose, 35.

9. *First Annual Report of the Boston Educational Commission for Freedmen* (Boston: Boston Educational Commission, 1863), 4; Rose, 35.

10. G. K. Eggleston, "The Work of Relief Societies during the Civil War," *Journal of Negro History* 14, no. 3 (July 1929): 273–274.

11. Ibid., 276–277.

12. *Freedmen's Record*, I, July 1865, 107.

13. Rose, 335.

14. Eggleston, 275–276.

15. *Second Annual Report of the New England Freedmen's Aid Society* (Boston, MA: Office of the New England Freedmen's Aid Society, 1864), 6.

16. New England Freedmen's Aid Society, *Circular*, October 20, 1865 (Boston, MA: New England Freedmen's Aid Society, 1865), 1.

17. Eggleston, 277.

18. *First Annual Report of the National Freedman's Relief Association* (New York: National Freedman's Relief Association, 1863), 1–2.

19. E. Allen Richardson, "Architects of a Benevolent Empire: The Relationship between the American Missionary Association and the Freedmen's Bureau in Virginia, 1865–1872," in *The Freedmen's Bureau and Reconstruction: Reconsiderations,* ed. Paul Cimbala and Randall Miller, 123 (New York: Fordham University Press, 1999).

20. Ibid., 122.

21. Eric Foner, *Reconstruction: America's Unfinished Revolution, 1863–1877* (New York: Harper and Row, 1988), 52.

22. Akiko Ochiai, "The Port Royal Experiment Revisited: Northern Visions of Reconstruction and the Land Question," *New England Quarterly* 74, no. 1 (March 2001): 106.

23. Ibid., 99.

24. *First Annual Report of the National Freedman's Relief Association,* 1.

25. Ibid., 2.

26. Isaac Brinckerhoff, *Advice to Freedmen* (New York: American Tract Society, 1864).

27. Nina Mjagkij, *Organizing Black America: An Encyclopedia of African American Associations* (New York: Routledge, 2001), 40–41.

28. Rose, 219.

29. Eggleston, 278; *First Annual Report of the National Freedman's Relief Association,* 5.

30. *Pennsylvania Freedmen's Relief Association Report, 1864,* 1–2. (Philadelphia: Pennsylvania Freedmen's Relief Association, 1864), 1

31. Eggleston, 278.

32. *Pennsylvania Freedmen's Relief Association Report, 1864,* 1–2.

33. *Pennsylvania Freedmen's Bulletin* 1, no. 1 (February 1865): 20.

34. *Pennsylvania Freedmen's Relief Association Report, 1864,* 1.

35. Rose, 76.

36. Eggleston, 280.

37. *Pennsylvania Freedmen's Relief Association Report, 1864,* 2.

38. Ibid., 2–3.

39. Eggleston, 280; Kurt Wolf, "Laura M. Towne and the Freed People of South Carolina, 1862–1901," *South Carolina Historical Magazine* 98, no. 4 (October 1997): 397.

40. Towne, 157.

41. Ibid., 140; Wolf, 396–397.

42. Wolf, 405.

43. Rose, 75.

44. Mjagkij, 40–41.

45. Ibid., 41.

46. Rose, 335.

47. Ibid., 374–376; Eggleston, 285–286; William McFeely, *Yankee Stepfather: General O. O. Howard and the Freedmen* (New York: W. W. Norton, 1994), 88–89; Mjagkij, 41.

48. McKim to Joseph Simpson, February 16, 1866, letterbook copy, McKim MSS, Cornell University, Ithaca, NY.

49. Rose, 375.

50. Laura Towne to McKim, March 26, 1866, McKim MSS.

51. Kay Ann Taylor, "Mary S. Peake and Charlotte L. Forten: Black Teachers during the Civil War and Reconstruction," *Journal of Negro Education* 74, no. 2 (Spring 2005): 125.

52. Rose, 40–41.

53. American Missionary Association, *History of the American Missionary Association: With Illustrative Facts and Anecdotes* (New York: The Association, 1891), 10. Hereafter AMA.

54. The 1872 AMA report quoted in John Rachal, "Gideonites and Freedmen: Adult Literacy Education at Port Royal, 1862–1865," *Journal of Negro Education* 55, no. 4 (Autumn 1986): 4, 59.

55. AMA, 10.

56. Ibid., 11–12.

57. Rose 26.

58. Ibid., 41.

59. Ibid., 219.

60. W. J. Richardson to George Whipple, May 21, 1864, uncatalogued box labeled "1862—A-J," American Missionary Society Archives, New Orleans, LA.

61. Richardson, 124.

62. Ibid. 119.

63. Rose, 333–334.

64. Ibid., 387–388; "Avery Institute," in *South Carolina Encyclopedia*, ed. Walter Edgar, 37 (Columbia: University of South Carolina Press, 2006).

65. Rose, xvi and 63.

66. David Davenport, "The New Diplomacy," *Policy Review* 116 (December 2002 and January 2003): 29–30.

67. Simmons, 83.

68. Francis Fukuyama, *Nation-Building: Beyond Afghanistan and Iraq* (Baltimore: The Johns Hopkins University Press, 2006), 241.

69. Rose, 180 and 278.

70. Ibid., xvii–xviii.

71. Towne, 135.

72. Peter Uvin et al., *Scaling Up NGO Programs in India: Strategies and Debates* (Boston: Institute for Development Research, 2000), 4–5.

73. Brown, 9.

74. Towne, 220. See also Wolf, 399.

75. 10th Mountain Division, *After Action Report* (Fort Drum, New York: Headquarters, 10th Mountain Division, 1993), i.

76. Elizabeth Ware Pearson, *Letters from Port Royal: Written at the Time of the Civil War* (Boston: W. B. Clarke, 1906), vi.

77. Rose, 336.

Chapter Four

1. Andy Sumner and Michael Tribe, *International Development Studies: Theories and Methods in Research and Practice* (Los Angeles: Sage, 2008), 10.

2. Robert Chambers, *Ideas for Development* (New York: Routledge, 2005), 185.

3. Ravi Kanbur, "What's Social Policy got to do with Economic Growth?," http://www.arts.cornell.edu/poverty/kanbur/SocPolEconGrowth.pdf (accessed June 23, 2011).

4. Lynnell Simonson and Virginia Bushaw, "Participatory Action Research: Easier Said Than Done," *American Sociologist* 24, no. 1 (Spring 1993): 28.

5. Sumner and Tribe, 38.

6. Foner, 51–52.

7. Ibid., 52.

8. Francis Fukuyama, *State-Building: Governance and World Order in the 21st Century* (Ithaca, NY: Cornell University Press, 2004), 55.

9. James Roark, *Masters without Slaves: Southern Planters in the Civil War and Reconstruction* (New York: W. W. Norton, 1977), 112

10. Rose, 43–44; Foner, 52.

11. Foner, 52.

12. Ibid., 29.

13. Ochiai, 106.

14. Ibid., 99.

15. Ibid., 96.

16. Foner, 51–54.

17. Rose, 226.

18. Andrew Natsios, "The Nine Principles of Reconstruction and Development," *Parameters* 35, no. 3 (Autumn 2005): 7.

19. Pierce, *Negroes*, 18.

20. Foner, 103.

21. Martin Abbott, "Free Land, Free Labor, and the Freedmen's Bureau," *Agricultural History* 30, no. 4 (October 1956): 150.

22. Pierce, 28.

23. Rose, 296. Land policy will be more fully discussed in subsequent chapters, including chapter 7, "Economic Development and Land Redistribution."

24. Pierce, 25; Rose, 33.

25. Rose, 19.

26. Ibid., 24–25.

27. Ibid., 164.

28. Austa French, *Slavery in South Carolina and the Ex-Slaves: Or The Port Royal Mission* (New York: Winchell French, 1862), 308.

29. Rose, 226.

30. Ibid., 224 and 227.

31. Ibid., 211–213.

32. Ibid., 213–214.

33. E. Pearson, 172 and 177; Rose, 214–215.

34. Rose, 215.

35. Towne, 106–107.

36. Towne, 129–130.

37. E. Pearson, 254.

38. Pease, 112.

39. Rose, 224.

40. Ibid., 307.

41. Ibid., 309.

42. Ibid., 309–310.

43. Ibid., 377.

44. Ochiai, 96.

45. Simonson and Bushaw, 28–29.

46. Sumner and Tribe, 142–144.

47. Simonson and Bushaw, 28.

48. Solon Barraclough, *Land Reform in Developing Countries: The Role of the State and Other Actors* (New York: United Nations Research Institute for Social Development, 1999), 9.

49. George Marshall, "Remarks by the Secretary of State at Harvard University on June 5, 1947," 7, George Marshall Foundation, Lexington, VA.

50. Natsios, 7.

51. Jeremi Suri, *Liberty's Surest Guardian* (New York: Free Press, 2011), 41.

52. Joshua Goldstein and Jon Pevehouse, *International Relations* (New York: Longman, 2010), 491.

53. Sumner and Tribe, 143–144.

54. Pierce, 8.

55. Simonson and Bushaw, 27.

56. Pierce, 8.

57. Ibid., 10.

58. Ibid., 14.

59. Foner, 97.

60. Pierce, 10.

61. Ibid., 11.

62. Ibid., 11.

63. Ibid., 17.

64. Ibid., 10.

65. Ibid., 10.

66. Julie Saville, *The Work of Reconstruction: From Slave to Wage Laborer in South Carolina, 1860–1870* (New York: Cambridge University Press, 1994), 56.

67. Bruce Berg, *Qualitative Research Methods for the Social Sciences* (Boston: Allyn and Bacon, 2001), 112.

68. Rose, 126.

69. William Sherman, *Memoirs*, vol. 2 (New York: D. Appleton, 1875), 247–248.

70. LaWanda Cox, "The Promise of Land for the Freedmen," *Mississippi Valley Historical Review* 45, no. 3 (December 1958): 429.

71. "Negroes of Savannah," New York Daily Tribune, February 13, 1865. Freedmen and Southern Society Project, http://www.history.umd.edu/Freedmen/savmtg.htm.

72. Cox, 430.

73. Oliver Howard, *Autobiography of Oliver Otis Howard*, vol. 2 (New York: Baker and Taylor, 1908), 189–190.

74. Rose, 353.

75. Pierce, 18.

76. Elizabeth Botume, *First Days among the Contrabands* (1893; New York: Lost Cause Press, 1968), 57.

77. Pease, 101.

78. Natsios, 7.

79. Wolf, 389–390.

80. Ibid., 399.

81. Rose, 203 and 85.

82. David Tucker, "Facing the Facts: The Failure of Nation Assistance," *Parameters* 23 (Summer 1993): 37.

83. Ilan Kapoor, "Participatory Development, Complicity, and Desire," *Third World Quarterly* 26, no. 8 (2005): 1217.

84. Jonathan Pugh, "Social Transformation and Participatory Planning in St. Lucia," *Royal Geographical Society* 37, no. 4 (December 2005): 385.

85. Ibid., 390.

86. Anthony Lake, Speech at George Washington University, March 1996, quoted in Stewart and Knaus, 116–117.

87. Natsios, 7.

88. Ochiai, 115.

89. Wolf, 400.

90. Simonson and Bushaw, 27; Natsios, 7.

Chapter Five

1. Dobbins, *Beginner's Guide*, 200.

2. "Secretary-General Describes Emerging Era in Global Affairs with Growing Role for Civil Society alongside Established Institutions," United Nations Press Release SG/SM 638, July 14, 1998, http://www.un.org/News/Press/docs/1998/19980714.sgsm6638.html.

3. Rose, 229.

4. Dobbins, *Beginner's Guide*, 200.

5. Rose, 315.

6. Pierce, "Freedmen," 24.

7. Ibid., 10 and 31–32.

8. Pierce, "Freedmen," 9.

9. Ibid., 9.

10. Pierce, *Negroes*, 28.

11. Pierce, "Freedmen," 9.

12. Ibid., 9–10.

13. Towne, 162.

14. Ibid., 92.

15. Rose, 219.

16. Towne, 127.

17. Ibid., 129.

18. Ibid., 177.

19. Ibid., 178.

20. Pierce, *Negroes*, 14.

21. Towne, 134.

22. Rose, 221–222.

23. Towne, 135.

24. Pierce, "Freedmen," 9.

25. Towne, 116.

26. Rose, 285–286.

27. Ibid., 222.

28. Roland Paris, *At War's End: Building Peace after Civil Conflict* (New York: Cambridge University Press, 2004), 194.

29. Dobbins, *Beginner's Guide*, 200.

30. Rose, 229.

31. Pease, 101.

32. Botume, 57

33. Rose, 88.

34. Ibid., 203.

35. Foner, 28–29; Rose, 38; Pierce, *Negroes*, 16.

36. *Beaufort Free South*, January 2, 1864.

37. Edward Atkinson, "The Reign of King Cotton," *Atlantic Monthly* 7 (April 1861): 454.

38. Rachal, 455.

39. Ibid., 465–466.

40. Ibid., 456.

41. Pierce, *Negroes*, 28; Rose, 88.

42. Pierce, *Negroes*, 36.

43. Richardson, 127.

44. Pierce, *Negroes*, 24.

45. *First Annual Report of the Boston Educational Commission for Freedmen* (Boston: Boston Educational Commission, 1863), 4.

46. Ray Allen Billington, ed., *The Journal of Charlotte L. Forten: A Free Negro in the Slave Era* (New York: W. W. Norton, 1981), 146.

47. Rose, 88.

48. Rachal, 459–460.

49. Towne, 27.

50. Ibid., 97.

51. Botume, 63.

52. Rachal, 461–463.

53. Ibid., 455.

54. Pierce, "Freedmen," 4. See also E. Pearson, 159.

55. Dobbins, *Beginner's Guide*, 202.

56. Rose, 233.

57. Ibid., 234.

58. Henry Lee Swint, *The Northern Teacher in the South, 1862–1870* (New York: Octagon Books, 1967), 73–74.

59. Towne, 220.

60. Dobbins, *Beginner's Guide*, 202.

61. "Avery Institute," 37; Wolf, 400.

62. Malcolm Knowles, *A History of the Adult Education Movement in the United States* (Huntington, NY: Robert E. Krieger, 1977), 75.

63. Kofi Annan, "Secretary-General Salutes International Workshop on Human Security in Mongolia," Two-Day Session in Ulaanbaatar, May 8–10, 2000. Press Release SG/SM/7382.

http://www.un.org/News/Press/docs/2000/20000508.sgsm7382.doc.html
08/27/01.

64. The Universal Declaration of Human Rights, Article 26, http://www
.un.org/en/documents/udhr/.

65. Atkinson, 454.

66. Rachel, 467.

67. Pierce, "Freedmen," 3.

68. Eggleston, 280.

69. Pennsylvania Freedmen's Relief Association, *Report* (Philadelphia: Merrihew and Thompson, 1863), 2.

70. Edward L. Pierce to L. Towne, April 19, 1868. Quoted in Wolf, 405.

71. Towne, 222.

72. Wolf, 404.

73. Ibid., 404.

74. Dobbins, *Beginner's Guide*, 202.

75. Towne, 220.

76. Wolf, 400.

77. Elizabeth Jacoway, *Yankee Missionaries in the South: The Penn School Experiment* (Baton Rouge: Louisiana State University Press, 1980), 31–32.

78. Howard Westwood, "Generals David Hunter and Rufus Saxton and Black Soldiers," *South Carolina Historical Magazine* 86, no. 3 (July 1985): 165.

79. Ibid., 166.

80. OR, ser. 1, 6:263–264; ibid, ser. 3, 2:292.

81. Westwood, 167.

82. OR, ser. 1, 6:176–177; ibid., ser. 3, 1:609–610, 626; ibid., ser. 3, 2:30; A. Howard Meneely, *The War Department, 1861* (New York, 1928), pp. 341–343.

83. OR, ser. 3, 2:29–31, 52.

84. For a brief history of emancipation, see Kevin Dougherty, *Encyclopedia of the Confederacy* (San Diego, CA: Thunder Bay Press, 2010), 104–105.

85. Rose, 145–146; Towne, 93–94.

86. OR, ser. 3, 2:60.

87. Pierce, "Freedmen," 27.

88. Towne, 94.

89. Westwood, 171.

90. Towne, 83–84; Westwood, 176.

91. OR, ser. 1, 14:377–378.

92. Westwood, 179.

93. Ibid., 165, and Dudley Cornish, *The Sable Arm: Black Troops in the Union Army, 1861–1865* (Lawrence: University Press of Kansas, 1987), 53.

94. Westwood, 177.

95. E. Pearson, 89.

96. Ibid., 93.

97. Towne, 93.

98. Ibid., 137.

99. Cornish, 104.

100. Ibid., 138.

101. E. Pearson, 153.

102. Towne, 107–108.

103. Quote from E. Pearson, 185. See ibid., 185, 188, 236, 239 as examples of squads firing on potential "recruits." See also Rose, 267.

104. E. Pearson, 175.

105. Pierce, "Freedmen," 27. See Rose, 269, for an alternative assessment of the recruiting procedures in 1864.

106. See Cornish, 88, for this characterization of Higginson.

107. Henry Greenleaf Pearson, *The Life of John A. Andrew: Governor of Massachusetts, 1861–1865* (Boston: Houghton, Mifflin, 1904), 2:70.

108. Pierce, "Freedmen," 27.

109. Poole, 93.

110. Rose, 270.

111. Thomas Higginson, *Army Life in a Black Regiment* (Cambridge, MA: Riverside Press, 1900), 64, quoted in Rose, 408.

112. Paris, 179.

113. E. Pearson, 267.

114. Ibid., 268. To Gannett's disappointment, the delegates were not received at the convention.

115. Towne, 183.

116. Ibid., 182–183.

117. Ibid., 183–184.

118. Ibid., 254.

119. Ibid., 114.

120. E. Pearson, 259.

121. Towne, 207.

122. Ibid., 216.

123. Ibid., 217.

124. Ibid., 269–270.

125. Andrew Billingsley, *Yearning to Breathe Free: Robert Smalls of South Carolina and His Families* (Columbia: University of South Carolina Press, 2007), 115–118 and 158. See chapter 8, "Political Development and Democratization," of this present book for a detailed discussion of the struggle for political control.

126. Rose, 229. See chapter 9, "Spoiler Problems and Resistance," of this present book for a detailed discussion of the restoration of white political control.

127. Donald Mitchell, *Cultural Geography: A Critical Introduction* (Oxford, UK: Blackwell, 2000), 136.

128. Definition from Dobbins, *Beginner's Guide*, 200.

129. Ibid., 200.

Chapter Six

1. The Office of the United Nations High Commissioner for Refugees, *The State of the World's Refugees: Human Displacement in the New Millennium* (New York: Oxford University Press, 2006), 1.

2. Poul Hartling, "Opening Statement" to Meeting of Experts on Refugee Aid and Development, Mont Pelerin, Switzerland, August 1983. Quoted in Barry Stein, "Durable Solutions for Developing Country Refugees," *International Migration Review* 20, no. 2 (Summer 1986): 264.

3. Pierce, *Negroes*, 5–6.

4. Botume, 16.

5. Pierce, *Negroes*, 5–6.

6. Towne, 73-75. The description of St. Helenaville is from Johnson, 110.

7. Botume, 35.

8. Ibid., 79. *The New Georgia Encyclopedia* concurs with this estimate. See http://www.georgiaencyclopedia.org/nge/Article.jsp?id=h-1084.

9. Rose, 320. See E. Pearson, 293, and Towne, 148–149, for descriptions of the conditions of the march.

10. Rose, 321.

11. Towne, 149.

12. Botume, 133.

13. Rose, 322.

14. Hermine Munz Baumhofer, "Economic Changes in St. Helena's Parish, 1860–1870," *South Carolina Historical and Genealogical Magazine* 50, no. 1 (January 1949): 6.

15. Michael Barutciski and Astri Suhrke, "Lessons from the Kosovo Refugee Crisis: Innovations in Protection and Burden Sharing," *Journal of Refugee Studies* 14, no. 2 (June 2001): 96.

16. Definitions of human security range from focusing on all the broad threats to personal well-being and dignity to specific challenges posed by political violence. The discussion in this chapter is primarily concerned with aspects of housing, the family, and child care. Other aspects of human security are discussed elsewhere, such as education in chapter 5. For general information on the concept of human security, see Amos Jordan et al., *American National Security* (Baltimore: The Johns Hopkins University Press, 2009), 4 and 548–551; Henry Nau, *Perspectives on International Relations* (Washington, DC: CQ Press, 2007), 26; Goldstein and Pevehouse, 425.

17. Pierce, *Negroes*, 7.

18. Towne, 57.

19. Ibid., 75.

20. E. Pearson, 77.

21. Rose, 107; Botume, 39–40; E. Pearson, 8.

22. Botume, 16.

23. Ibid., 50–51.

24. Ibid., 52.

25. Ibid., 51 and 62.

26. Ibid., 56.

27. Rose, 20.

28. Pierce, *Negroes*, 22–23.

29. Botume, 67.

30. Ibid., 57.

31. Marian Zeitlin et al., *Strengthening the Family—Implications for International Development* (New York: United Nations University Press, 1995), 1.

32. Rose, 238–239.

33. John Blassingame, *The Slave Community: Plantation Life in the Antebellum South* (New York: Oxford University Press, 1979), 165.

34. Ann Garry and Marilyn Pearsall, *Women, Knowledge, and Reality: Explorations in Feminist Philosophy* (New York: Routledge, 1996), 469; Rose, 89.

35. Towne, 24.

36. Pierce, "Freedmen," 6.

37. Ibid., 6.

38. Edward Miller, *Gullah Statesman: Robert Smalls from Slavery to Congress, 1839–1915* (Columbia: University of South Carolina Press, 1995), 8.

39. Jacoway, 29.

40. Pierce, "Freedmen," 6.

41. Ibid., 13.

42. Ibid., 12–13, notes it was "a rare exception on which the white family has not contributed to populate the negro houses."

43. Jacoway, 29.

44. Pierce, *Negroes*, 7.

45. Rose, 134.

46. Ibid., 135.

47. Pierce, "Freedmen," 5.

48. Before this act was passed by Congress, every state except South Carolina had already made the slave trade illegal. See John Blum et al., *The National Experience: A History of the United States* (New York: Harcourt Brace Jovanovich College Publishers, 1993), 178.

49. Pierce, "Freedmen," 6.

50. Towne, 24–25.

51. Nehemiah Adams, *A South-Side View of Slavery* (Boston: T. R. Marvin, 1854), 85

52. Towne, 184.

53. Pierce, "Freedmen," 6. Johnson, 98, reminds that the "infant death rate among whites was also high."

54. Pierce, "Freedmen," 6.

55. Rose, 236 and 138.

56. Marriage Records of the Office of the Commissioner, *Washington Headquarters of the Bureau of Refugees, Freedmen, and Abandoned Lands, 1861–1869* (Washington, DC: United States Congress and National Archives and Records Administration, 2002), 6.

57. Pierce, "Freedmen," 25.

58. Ibid., 14.

59. See, for example, Joint Publication 3-07, *Joint Doctrine for Military Operations Other Than War* (Washington, DC: Joint Chiefs of Staff, 1995), II-4, II-5.

60. Pierce, "Freedmen," 7.

61. Ibid., 7.

62. Botume, 66.

63. E. Pearson, 294.

64. Towne, 148.

65. Ibid., 148–149.

66. William Sherman, *Memoirs of General William T. Sherman*, vol. 2 (New York: D. Appleton, 1875), 240.

67. Special Field Orders, No. 15, Headquarters Military Division of the Mississippi, January 16, 1865, Orders and Circulars, ser. 44, Adjutant General's Office, Record Group 94, National Archives, Washington, DC.

68. Sherman, 250.

69. Rose, 332.

70. Alexia Jones Helsley, *Beaufort, South Carolina: A History* (Charleston, SC: The History Press, 2005), 116.

71. Joint Publication 3-07.6, *Joint Tactics, Techniques, and Procedures for Foreign Humanitarian Assistance* (Washington, DC: Chairman of the Joint Chiefs of Staff, 2001), IV-8.

72. Walter Fleming, "Forty Acres and a Mule," *North American Review* 182 (May 1906): 728. The process by which much of the land was restored to its previous white owners will be more thoroughly discussed in chapter 9, "Spoiler Problems and Resistance."

73. *New York Times*, October 8, 1862, 1. Quoted in Michael Trinkley and Debi Hacker, *The Archaeological Manifestations of the "Port Royal Experiment" at*

Mitchelville, Hilton Head, South Carolina (Columbia, SC: Chicora Foundation, 1987), 4.

74. Joseph Danielson, *War's Desolating Scourge: The Union's Occupation of Northern Alabama* (Lawrence: University Press of Kansas, 2012), 79–81.

75. Trinkley and Hacker, 4. See also Phineas Camp Headley, *The Patriot Boy: or, The Life and Career of Major-General Ormsby M. Mitchel* (New York: W. H. Appleton, 1865), 256.

76. Trinkley and Hacker, 4; Martin Abbott, "Freedom's Cry: Negroes and Their Meetings in South Carolina, 1865–1869," *Phylon Quarterly* 20, no. 3 (3rd Quarter 1959): 266. Hereafter Abbott "Freedom's Cry."

77. Sherman, 246.

78. Trinkley and Hacker, 5.

79. Ibid., 5.

80. *The Civil War, Hilton Head, and the Evolution of Mitchelville* (Columbia, SC: Chicora Foundation, 1995), 8–10.

81. Congressional Reports: H.R. Rep. 109-377, *A Failure of Initiative: Final Report of the Select Bipartisan Committee to Investigate the Preparation for and Response to Hurricane Katrina* (Washington, DC: U.S. Government Printing Office, 2006), 312.

82. Karen Bogenschneider, *Family Policy Matters: How Policymaking Affects Families and What Professionals Can Do* (Mahwah, NJ: Lawrence Erlbaum Associates, 2002), 41–48.

83. Ibid., 48.

84. French, 53.

85. Bogenschneider, 89–90.

86. *Beaufort Free South*, January 2, 1864; Bogenschneider, 94.

87. Bogenschneider, 110.

88. Ibid., 37–38.

89. Pierce, "Freedmen," 4.

90. Rachal, 462–463.

91. Bogenschneider, 238.

Chapter Seven

1. Pierce, *Negroes*, 23.

2. Beale, Howard, ed., *The Diary of Edward Bates, 1859–1866* (Washington DC: Government Printing Office, 1933), 194–195.

3. Pierce, *Negroes*, 7.

4. Dobbins, *Beginner's Guide*, 167.

5. Rose, 19.

6. Beale, 207.

7. Rose, 204–205; Pierce, *Negroes*, 14.

8. Pierce, *Negroes*, 17.

9. Ibid., 18.

10. Martin Abbott, *The Freedmen's Bureau in South Carolina, 1865–1872* (Chapel Hill: University of North Carolina Press, 1967), 12.

11. "Democrats: Bush Downplaying Iraq Costs," CNN Politics, April 15, 2004, http://articles.cnn.com/2004-04-15/politics/bush.oil_1_oil-revenues-oil-fields-iraq-war?_s=PM:ALLPOLITICS.

12. See Deborah Avant, "The Privatization of Security: Lessons from Iraq," *Orbis* 50, no. 2 (Spring 2006): 327–342, for one of the more balanced accounts of the use of contractors.

13. Stewart and Knaus, 8.

14. E. Pearson, 254.

15. Rose, 224.

16. Ibid., 227.

17. Cox, 435–436.

18. Chambers, 185.

19. Ochiai, 96.

20. See Robert Darnton, "The Pursuit of Happiness," *Wilson Quarterly* 19, no. 4 (Autumn 1995): 43, for this interpretation of the Enlightenment understanding of happiness.

21. Stewart and Knaus, 59.

22. See Jared Diamond, *Guns, Germs, and Steel: The Fates of Human Societies* (New York: W. W. Norton, 1999), 18; Richard Easterlin, "Building a Better Theory of Well-Being," in *Economics and Happiness: Framing the Analysis*, ed. Luigino Bruni and Pier Luigi Porta, 29–64 (New York: Oxford University Press, 2005); and Tony Waters, *The Persistence of Subsistence Agriculture: Life Beneath the Level of the Marketplace* (Lanham, MD: Lexington Books, 2006).

23. Vandana Shiva, *Staying Alive: Women, Ecology, and Development* (London: Zed Books, 1988), 10.

24. Foner, 51–54; Rose, 226.

25. Foner, 103.

26. Quoted on a sign at Fish Haul Creek Park, Hilton Head, South Carolina.

27. Abbott, "Free Land," 204.

28. Hermine Munz Baumhofer, "Economic Changes in St. Helena's Parish, 1860–1870," *South Carolina Historical and Genealogical Magazine* 50, no. 1 (January 1949), 2.

29. Cox, 435.

30. Ochiai, 96.

31. Barraclough, 48.

32. *Pennsylvania Freedmen's Bulletin* 1, no. 1 (February 1865): 20.

33. Barraclough, 48.

34. Pierce, *Negroes*, 28.

35. Ochiai, 96.

36. Rose, 226; Ochiai, 99.

37. E. Pearson, 148.

38. Rose, 164.

39. French, 308.

40. Rose, 224 and 227.

41. Ochiai, 97–99.

42. Rose, 49.

43. W. C. Gannett to E. S. Gannett, March 14, [1862], William Channing Gannett Collection, in the possession of Louis S. Garnett, West Cornwall, CT, quoted in Pease, 99.

44. Rose, 68.

45. Ibid., 128 and 213.

46. Ibid., 128.

47. Ibid., 205.

48. Ibid., 82–83 and 224–225.

49. E. Pearson, 111.

50. Ibid., 119.

51. Ibid., 140 and note on 140–141. See also Rose, 212–213.

52. E. Pearson, 172 and 177; Rose, 214–215.

53. Rose, 281.

54. Ochiai, 99–100.

55. Rose, 215; Goldstein and Pevehouse, 473.

56. Rose, 226.

57. E. Pearson, 274.

58. Goldstein and Pevehouse, 473.

59. Cox, 436.

60. Ochiai, 101–102, 113.

61. Ibid., 107.

62. Frederick J. Williams, column in *Beaufort Free South*, n.d., reprinted in *Liberator*, March 11, 1864, quoted in Ochiai, 108.

63. Ochiai, 108.

64. Barraclough, 1.

65. Ochiai, 117.

66. Goldstein and Pevehouse, 473; Rose, 309.

67. Ochiai, 117.

68. Ibid., 108–109.

69. E. Pearson, 277.

70. Foner, 53.

71. Ochiai, 113.

72. Pease, 111.

73. E. Pearson, 254.

74. Ochiai, 114.

75. Special Field Orders, No. 15, Headquarters Military Division of the Mississippi, January 16, 1865, Orders and Circulars, ser. 44, Adjutant General's Office, Record Group 94, National Archives, Washington, DC.

76. Rose, 357; Foner, 161; Abbott, *Freedmen's Bureau*, 16, 127–128.

77. Abbott, *Freedman's Bureau*, 80–81.

78. See, for example, John Coakley and Michael Gallagher, *Politics in the Republic of Ireland* (New York: Routledge, 1999), 99.

79. Samuel Huntington, *Political Order in Changing Societies* (New Haven, CT: Yale University Press, 2006), 299.

80. Barraclough, 1.

81. Ibid., 1.

82. David Donald, *Charles Sumner and the Rights of Man* (New York: Knopf, 1970), 299.

83. Foner, 214.

84. Ibid., 214.

85. Huntington, 299.

86. Goldstein and Pevehouse, 473.

87. Rose, 296.

88. Ibid., 296.

89. Joint Pub 1-02, *Department of Defense Dictionary of Military and Associated Terms* (Washington, DC: Joint Chiefs of Staff, 2010), 289.

90. Pierce, "Freedmen," 23.

91. Ibid., 24.

92. John Martin Davis, "Bankless in Beaufort: A Reexamination of the 1873 Failure of the Freedman's Savings Branch at Beaufort," *South Carolina Historical Magazine* 104, no. 1 (January 2003): 40.

93. See Shon McCormick, "A Primer on Developing Measures of Effectiveness," *Military Review* (July–August 2010): 60–66, for the continuing difficulty the military has in determining MOEs that measure largely qualitative factors, and James Wilson Gibson, *The Perfect War: Technology in Vietnam* (Boston: Atlantic Monthly Press, 1986), for a discussion of the specific difficulties experienced in the Vietnam War.

94. Pierce, Negroes, 25.

95. Huntington, 53–54.

96. Pierce, Negroes, 12.

97. Rose, 369.

98. Mary Ames, *From a New England Woman's Diary in Dixie in 1865* (Springfield, MA: Plimpton Press, 1906), 8.

99. Huntington, 53–54.

100. E. Pearson, 254–255.

101. J. T. Trowbridge, *The South: A Tour of Its Battlefields and Ruined Cities* (Hartford, CT, 1866), 545.

102. Ibid., 264. For Philbrick's response, see E. Pearson, 266–267.

103. Quoted in Rose, 313.

104. Rose, 357. See also Abbott, *Freedmen's Bureau*, 72–73, for additional commentary on the black response.

105. Rose, 362–363.

106. James Fearon and David Laitin, "Neotrusteeship and the Problem of Weak States," *International Security* 28, no. 4 (Spring 2004): 43.

107. Tryon Edwards, *A Dictionary of Thoughts: Being a Cyclopedia of Laconic Quotations from the Best Authors of the World, Both Ancient and Modern* (Detroit: F. B. Dickerson, 1908), 80.

108. Rose, 182.

109. Ibid., 381.

110. Baumhofer, 9.

111. Ibid., 13.

Chapter Eight

1. Carl von Clausewitz, *On War*, ed. Michael Howard and Peter Paret, 87 (Princeton, NJ: Princeton University Press, 1984).

2. "A Letter from President Lincoln; Reply to Horace Greeley. Slavery and the Union. The Restoration of the Union the Paramount Object," *New York Times*, August 24, 1862.

3. Roland Paris, *At War's End: Building Peace after Civil Conflict* (New York: Cambridge University Press, 2004), 191–192.

4. *Columbia Daily Phoenix* (South Carolina), September 23, 1865.

5. *Journal of the Convention of the People of South Carolina: Held in Columbia, S.C., September, 1865* (Columbia, SC: J. A. Shelby, 1865), 14–15.

6. *Journal of the Convention*, 103.

7. Richard Zuczek, *State of Rebellion: Reconstruction in South Carolina* (Columbia: University of South Carolina Press, 1996), 15.

8. Dan Carter, *When the War Was Over: The Failure of Self-Reconstruction in the South, 1865–1867* (Baton Rouge: Louisiana State University Press, 1985), 177; Zuczek, 16.

9. The first quote is from the *New York Tribune*, April 15, 1866, cited in Zuczek, 36–37, from a reprint of the *New York Herald* in Greenville *Southern Enterprise* (South Carolina), January 31, 1867. The second is from the *New York Tribune*,

April 15, 1866, cited in Lilian Kibler, *Benjamin F. Perry: South Carolina Unionist* (Durham, NC: Duke University Press, 1946), 446.

10. *New York Tribune*, April 15, 1866, cited in Zuczek, 37.

11. *New York Tribune*, September 22, 1866, cited in Kibler, 411.

12. Zuczek, 39.

13. Ibid., 39–42 and 50.

14. Ibid., 48–51.

15. Simon Bolivar, "Reply of a South American to a Gentleman of this Island," in *Selected Writings of Bolivar*, trans. Lewis Bertrand, 110 (New York: The Colonial Press, 1951).

16. Zuczek, 42.

17. Miller, 42; Rose, 229. See also chapter 5, "The Development of Civil Society," in this present book.

18. Miller, 42; Foner, 110.

19. Miller, 9–12.

20. Ibid., 12.

21. Ibid., 15.

22. Ibid., 27.

23. Ibid., 41.

24. Billingsley, 104.

25. Dobbins, *Beginner's Guide*, 197 and 207.

26. L. Earnest Sellers, "Robert Smalls: Civil War Hero," *Negro Digest* (April 1964): 27.

27. Miller, 41.

28. Billingsley, 104–105 and 22.

29. Ibid., 27 and 105.

30. Thomas Holt, *Black over White: Negro Political Leadership in South Carolina during Reconstruction* (Urbana: University of Illinois Press, 1977), 47.

31. Billingsley, 103–104; Sellers, 27.

32. Paris, 188. For a detailed discussion of Smalls's political career, the reader is recommended to consult Edward Miller's *Gullah Statesman: Robert Smalls from Slavery to Congress, 1839–1915* (University of South Carolina Press, 1995).

33. Dobbins, *Beginner's Guide*, 199.

34. Hampton to John Mullaly, March 31, 1867, in *Family Letters of the Three Wade Hamptons, 1782–1901*, ed. Charles Cauthen, 141–143 (Columbia: University of South Carolina Press, 1953).

35. Rod Andrew, Wade Hampton: Confederate Warrior to Southern Redeemer (Chapel Hill: University of North Carolina Press, 2008), 337

36. *Charleston Daily Courier*, March 23, 1867, 1.

37. Robert Levine, *Martin R. Delany: A Documentary Reader* (Chapel Hill: University of North Carolina Press, 2003), 380–381.

38. Andrew, 337.

39. Stephen Stedman, "Spoiler Problems in Peace Processes," *International Security* 22, no. 2 (Fall 1997): 10. This and other aspects of Stedman's spoiler theory are the subject of chapter 9, "Spoiler Problems and Resistance," of this present book.

40. John Mearsheimer, "The Only Exit from Bosnia," *New York Times*, October 7, 1997, A31.

41. Samuel Huntington, "Democracy's Third Wave," *Journal of Democracy* 2, no. 2 (Spring 1991): 17–18. See also Samuel Huntington, *The Third Wave: Democratization in the Late 20th Century* (Norman: University of Oklahoma Press, 1991).

42. Jeffrey Pickering and Mark Peceny, "Forging Democracy at Gunpoint," *International Studies Quarterly* 50 (2006): 540.

43. Ibid., 540–542.

44. Ibid., 554.

Chapter Nine

1. Stedman, 8.

2. Ibid., 5.

3. Ibid., 17.

4. Stewart and Knaus, 128.

5. Ibid., 151.

6. Ibid., 148.

7. Stedman, 12.

8. Ibid., 6.

9. Ibid., 25.

10. Rose, 19.

11. Pierce, *Negroes*, 29.

12. Towne, 102–103. See also Rose, 240.

13. Rose, 27.

14. OR, series III, vol. 2, 27.

15. Rose, 153–154.

16. James Schmidt, "'A Full-Fledged Government of Men': Freedmen's Bureau Labor Policy in South Carolina, 1865–1868," in *The Freedmen's Bureau and Reconstruction: Reconsiderations*, ed. Paul Cimbala and Randall Miller, 224–225 (New York: Fordham University Press, 1999).

17. Rose, 178.

18. Towne, 88; Rose, 178–179.

19. OR, series III, vol. 55, 1030–1031.

20. Schmidt, 221.

21. McFeely, 62–63.

22. Schmidt, 221.

23. Ezra Warner, *Generals in Blue: Lives of the Union Commanders* (Baton Rouge: Louisiana State University Press, 1964), 238.

24. Stedman, 8.

25. Ibid, 8.

26. Rose, 67.

27. Pierce, *Negroes*, 35.

28. Rose, 67–69.

29. Towne, 60.

30. Stedman, 8.

31. Rose, 142.

32. Ibid., 143.

33. Schmidt, 220.

34. Ibid., 235.

35. Stedman, 8.

36. Zuczek, 55.

37. Ibid., 55.

38. Foner, 26.

39. Ibid., 425–426.

40. Zuczek, 170; Francis Simkins and Robert Woody, *South Carolina during Reconstruction* (Chapel Hill: University of North Carolina Press, 1932), 503.

41. Zuczek, 169–170.

42. W. Scott Poole, "Religion, Gender, and the Lost Cause in South Carolina's 1876 Governor's Race: 'Hampton or Hell!'" *Journal of Southern History* 68, no. 3 (August, 2002): 574.

43. Philip Dray, *Capitol Men: The Epic Story of Reconstruction through the Lives of the First Black Congressmen* (New York: Houghton Mifflin Harcourt, 2008), 306.

44. Stedman, 9.

45. Ochiai, 97–99.

46. E. Pearson, 248.

47. Ochiai, 101–102, 113.

48. Ibid., 104.

49. Ibid., 113.

50. Ibid., 114.

51. Towne, 178.

52. Saville, 73.

53. McFeely, 94.

54. Ibid., 134; Saville, 80–81.

55. Endorsement of Saxton on a petition from Constantine Bailey, September 26, 1865, quoted in Abbott, "Free Land," 152.

56. Rose, 350.

57. Stedman, 9.

58. George Bentley, *A History of the Freedmen's Bureau* (Philadelphia: University of Pennsylvania, 1955), 98; Rose, 352–353.

59. McFeely, 128.

60. Rose, 357; Foner, 161; Abbott, *Freedmen's Bureau*, 16, 127–128.

61. Stedman, 17.

62. Roark, 112.

63. McFeely, 55.

64. Rose, 360.

65. Ibid., 374–376; Eggleston, 285–286; McFeely, 88–89; Mjagkij, 41.

66. McKim to Joseph Simpson, February 16, 1866, letterbook copy, McKim MSS, quoted in Rose, 375.

67. Abbott, *Freedmen's Bureau*, 128–129.

68. Ibid., 129.

69. Stedman, 10.

70. Kelly Greenhill and Solomon Major, "The Perils of Profiling: Civil War Spoilers and the Collapse of Intrastate Accords," *International Security* 31, no. 3 (Winter 2006–2007): 8.

71. Ibid., 38–39.

72. Ibid., 9.

73. Zuczek, 77.

74. Andrew, 367.

75. Greenhill and Major, 9; Wade Hampton to James Connor, April 11, 1869, in Box 5, Hampton Family Papers, South Caroliniana Library, University of South Carolina, Columbia, SC, quoted in Zuczek, 77.

76. Andrew, 386.

77. Zuczek, 197.

78. Greenhill and Major, 9.

79. Zuczek, 197–198.

80. Ulysses S. Grant, in *New York Tribune*, February 18, 1877, quoted in Zuczek, 198.

81. Greenhill and Major, 13.

82. See Francis Simkins, "The Ku Klux Klan in South Carolina, 1868–1871," *Journal of Negro History* 12, no. 4 (October 1927): 606–647.

83. Alfred Williams, "General Wade Hampton Campaigns in the 'Black Belt,'" in) *Port Royal under Six Flags*, ed. Katharine Jones, 315 and 316 (Indianapolis, IN: Bobbs-Merrill, 1960).

84. Towne, 289.

85. Dray, 306 and 309.

86. Stedman, 10.

87. Rose, 359.

88. Towne, 163.

89. New York *Nation*, November 30, 1865, quoted in E. Pearson, 320.

90. Rose, 348–349.

91. T. E. R. to C. P. W., St. Helena, May 6, 1865, in E. Pearson, 311.

92. Towne, 163.

93. Ibid., 167.

94. Rose, 224 and 227.

95. McFeely, 53.

96. Pierce, 25.

97. Rose, 215.

98. Towne, 106–107; E. Pearson, 276.

99. Rose, 309–310.

100. Ibid., 377.

101. Herbert Shapiro, "The Ku Klux Klan during Reconstruction: The South Carolina Episode," *Journal of Negro History* 49, no. 1 (January 1964): 54–55.

102. Stedman, 48.

103. Abbott, *Freedmen's Bureau*, 11.

104. Ibid., 12.

105. Ibid., 132.

106. Ibid., 21.

107. H. G. Judd, "Report Concerning Freedmen on Port Royal and Adjacent Islands," August 1, 1865, National Archives Microfilm Publication M869 Roll 34.

108. Correspondence between Saxton and Gillmore, October 25–26, 1865, Bureau Records, SC, Box 473, quoted in Abbott, *Freedmen's Bureau*, 13.

109. Abbott, *Freedmen's Bureau*, 20.

110. Randall Miller, "Introduction. The Freedmen's Bureau and Reconstruction: An Overview," in *The Freedmen's Bureau and Reconstruction: Reconsiderations*, ed. Paul Cimbala and Randall Miller, xxix (New York: Fordham University Press, 1999).

111. Rose, 196.

112. Annual Report of Scott, November 1, 1866, Bureau Records, Box 778, quoted in Abbott, *Freedmen's Bureau*, 26.

113. Rufus Saxton to O. O. Howard, September 8, 1865, quoted in McFeely, 129.

114. Report to the Assistant Adjutant General, October 7, 1872, House Executive Documents, 42rd Cong., 3rd Sess., no. 109 (serial 1566), cited in Abbott, *Freedmen's Bureau*, 22.

115. Miller, xxv.

116. Zuczek, 210.

117. Stedman, 12.

118. Ibid., 12.

119. Ibid., 13.

120. Ibid., 13.

121. Ibid., 7.

122. Ibid., 15.

123. Greenhill and Major, 12.

124. Stedman, 15.

125. Ibid., 15.

Chapter Ten

1. David Tucker, "Facing the Facts: The Failure of Nation Assistance," *Parameters* 23 (Summer 1993): 34.

2. Paul Miller, "The Case for Nation-Building: Why and How to Fix Failed States," *Prism* 3, no. 1 (December 2011): 68.

3. Stewart and Knaus, xvii–xviii.

4. Ibid., xix–xxvi.

5. Ibid., xxiv.

6. Ibid., xxv.

7. Suri, 41.

8. Ibid., 77–78.

9. Lenny Smith, *Chaos: A Very Short Introduction* (New York: Oxford University Press, 2007), 164.

10. Pickering and Peceny, 556.

11. Fukuyama, *State-Building*, 100.

12. Ibid., 100.

13. Ibid., 37.

14. Ibid., 100.

15. Ibid., 38.

16. Ibid., 101.

17. Ibid., 19.

18. Ibid., 7.

19. Ibid., 7.

20. Dan Reiter, "Does Peace Nurture Democracy?," *Journal of Politics* 63, no. 3 (August 2001): 936.

21. Ibid, 936.

22. Fukuyama, *State-Building*, 21.

23. Paris, 187–188.

24. Ibid., 188.

25. Ibid., 189.

26. Ibid., 189–190.

27. Ibid., 193.

28. Ibid., 192.

29. Edward King, *The Southern States of North America: A Record of Journeys in Louisiana, Texas, the Indian Territory, Missouri, Arkansas, Mississippi, Alabama, Georgia, Florida, South Carolina, North Carolina, Kentucky, Tennessee, Virginia, West Virginia, and Maryland*, vol. 1 (Hartford, CT: American Publishing Company, 1875), 462.

30. Rachal, 468.

31. Paris, 196.

32. Ibid., 199.

33. See Chalmers Johnson, *MITI and the Japanese Miracle: The Growth of Industrial Policy, 1925–1975* (Palo Alto, CA: Stanford University Press, 1982).

34. Chalmers Johnson, *Japan: Who Governs?: The Rise of the Developmental State* (New York: W. W. Norton, 1994), 28–29.

35. Davis, 27.

36. Johnson, 28–29.

37. Davis, 50.

38. Paris, 207.

39. Ibid., 188.

40. Ibid., 208 and 210.

41. Rose, 389. She references commentary by King, 602, although King's assessment is not quite as directly worded as Rose's.

42. Edward Mansfield and Jack Snyder, "The Sequencing 'Fallacy,'" *Journal of Democracy* 18, no. 3 (July 2007): 6.

43. Ibid., 7.

44. Ibid., 7.

45. Samuel Huntington, *Political Order in Changing Societies* (New Haven, CT: Yale University Press, 1968), 227–228.

46. Ibid., 262.

47. Ibid., 7–8.

48. Paris, 207.

49. Stewart and Knaus, 40.

50. Huntington, 8.

51. Francis Fukuyama, "Liberalism versus State-Building," *Journal of Democracy* 18, no. 3 (July 2007): 11.

52. Fearon and Laitin, 21.

53. Rose, 389.

54. Pierce, *Negroes*, 25.

55. Rose, 381.

56. Ibid., 384.

57. Towne, 235.

58. Mansfield and Snyder, 6.

59. Thomas Carothers, "How Democracies Emerge: The 'Sequencing' Fallacy," *Journal of Democracy* 18, no. 1 (January 2007): 22.

60. Stewart and Knaus, 71.

61. Fukuyama, *State-Building*, 100.

Bibliography

Abbott, Martin. "Free Land, Free Labor, and the Freedmen's Bureau." *Agricultural History* 30, no. 4 (1956): 150–156.

Abbott, Martin. "Freedom's Cry: Negroes and Their Meetings in South Carolina, 1865–1869." *Phylon Quarterly* 20, no. 3 (1959): 263–272.

Abbott, Martin. *The Freedmen's Bureau in South Carolina, 1865–1872.* Chapel Hill: University of North Carolina Press, 1967.

Adams, Nehemiah. *A South-Side View of Slavery.* Boston: T. R. Marvin, 1854.

Allard, Kenneth. *Somalia Operations: Lessons Learned.* Washington, DC: National Defense University Press, 1995.

American Missionary Association. *History of the American Missionary Association: With Illustrative Facts and Anecdotes.* New York: The Association, 1891.

Ames, Mary. *From a New England Woman's Diary in Dixie in 1865.* Springfield, MA: Plimpton Press, 1906.

Anderson, Bern. *By Sea and By River: A Naval History of the Civil War.* Westport, CT: Greenwood Press, 1962.

Andrew, Rod. *Wade Hampton: Confederate Warrior to Southern Redeemer.* Chapel Hill: University of North Carolina Press, 2008.

Atkinson, Edward. "The Reign of King Cotton." *Atlantic Monthly* 7 (April 1861): 450–465.

"Avery Institute." In *South Carolina Encyclopedia,* ed. Walter Edgar. Columbia: University of South Carolina Press, 2006.

Barraclough, Solon. *Land Reform in Developing Countries: The Role of the State and Other Actors.* New York: United Nations Research Institute for Social Development, 1999.

Barutciski, Michael, and Astri Suhrke. "Lessons from the Kosovo Refugee Crisis: Innovations in Protection and Burden Sharing." *Journal of Refugee Studies* 14, no. 2 (2001): 95–134.

Baumhofer, Hermine Munz. "Economic Changes in St. Helena's Parish, 1860–1870." *South Carolina Historical and Genealogical Magazine* 50, no. 1 (January 1949): 1–13.

Beale, Howard, ed. *The Diary of Edward Bates, 1859–1866.* Washington, DC: Government Printing Office, 1933.

Bentley, George. *A History of the Freedmen's Bureau*. Philadelphia: University of Pennsylvania, 1955.

Berg, Bruce. *Qualitative Research Methods for the Social Sciences*. Boston: Allyn and Bacon, 2001.

Billingsley, Andrew. *Yearning to Breathe Free: Robert Smalls of South Carolina and His Families*. Columbia: University of South Carolina Press, 2007.

Blassingame, John. *The Slave Community: Plantation Life in the Antebellum South*. New York: Oxford University Press, 1979.

Blum, John et al. *The National Experience*. New York: Harcourt, Brace, and Jovanovich, 1993.

Bogenschneider, Karen. *Family Policy Matters: How Policymaking Affects Families and What Professionals Can Do*. Mahwah, N.J.: Lawrence Erlbaum Associates, 2002.

Botume, Elizabeth. *First Days among the Contrabands*. New York: Lee and Shepard, 1893.

Brinckerhoff, Isaac. *Advice to Freedmen*. New York: American Tract Society, 1864.

Brooks, Elaine. "Massachusetts Anti-Slavery Society." *Journal of Negro History* 30, no. 3 (July 1945): 311–330.

Brown, Philip, and Jessica Minty. *Media Coverage & Charitable Giving after the 2004 Tsunami*. Ann Arbor, MI: William Davidson Institute, 2006.

Carothers, Thomas. "How Democracies Emerge: The 'Sequencing' Fallacy." *Journal of Democracy* 18, no. 1 (January 2007): 12–27.

Carter, Dan. *When the War Was Over: The Failure of Self-Reconstruction in the South, 1865–1867*. Baton Rouge: Louisiana State University Press, 1985.

Catton, Bruce. *This Hallowed Ground*. Garden City, NY: Doubleday, 1956.

Cauthen, Charles, ed. *Family Letters of the Three Wade Hamptons, 1782–1901*. Columbia: University of South Carolina Press, 1953.

Chaitin, Peter. *The Coastal War*. Alexandria, VA: Time-Life Books, 1984.

Chambers, Robert. *Ideas for Development*. New York: Routledge, 2005.

The Civil War, Hilton Head, and the Evolution of Mitchelville. Columbia, SC: Chicora Foundation, 1995.

Clausewitz, Carl von. *On War*. Edited by Michael Howard and Peter Paret. Princeton, NJ: Princeton University Press, 1984.

Coakley, John, and Michael Gallagher. *Politics in the Republic of Ireland*. New York: Routledge, 1999.

Cox, LaWanda. "The Promise of Land for the Freedmen." *Mississippi Valley Historical Review* 45, no. 3 (December 1958): 413–440.

Danielson, Joseph. *War's Desolating Scourge: The Union's Occupation of Northern Alabama*. Lawrence: University Press of Kansas, 2012.

Darnton, Robert. "The Pursuit of Happiness." *The Wilson Quarterly* 19, no. 4 (Autumn 1995): 42–52.

Davenport, David. "The New Diplomacy." *Policy Review* 116 (December 2002 and January 2003): 17–30.

Davis, John Martin. "Bankless in Beaufort: A Reexamination of the 1873 Failure of the Freedman's Savings Branch at Beaufort." *South Carolina Historical Magazine* 104, no. 1 (January 2003): 25–55.

Diamond, Jared. *Guns, Germs, and Steel: The Fates of Human Societies.* New York: W. W. Norton, 1999.

Dobbins, James. *America's Role in Nation-Building: From Germany to Iraq.* Santa Monica, CA: RAND, 2003.

Dobbins, James et al. *The Beginner's Guide to Nation-Building.* Santa Monica, CA: RAND, 2007.

Donald, David. *Charles Sumner and the Rights of Man.* New York: Knopf, 1970.

Donald, David, ed. *Inside Lincoln's Cabinet, The Civil War Diaries of Salmon P. Chase.* New York: Longman's, Green, 1954.

Dougherty, Kevin. *Strangling the Confederacy.* Philadelphia: Casemate, 2010.

Dray, Philip. *Capitol Men: The Epic Story of Reconstruction through the Lives of the First Black Congressmen.* New York: Houghton Mifflin Harcourt, 2008.

Dworken, Jonathan. "Restore Hope: Coordinating Relief Operations." *Joint Forces Quarterly* 8 (Summer 1995): 14–20.

Easterlin, Richard. "Building a Better Theory of Well-Being." In *Economics and Happiness: Framing the Analysis*, ed. Luigino Bruni and Pier Luigi Porta, 29–64. New York: Oxford University Press, 2005.

Edwards, Tryon. *A Dictionary of Thoughts: Being a Cyclopedia of Laconic Quotations from the Best Authors of the World, Both Ancient and Modern.* Detroit: F. B. Dickerson Co., 1908.

Eggleston, G. K. "The Work of Relief Societies during the Civil War." *Journal of Negro History* 14, no. 3 (July 1929): 272–299.

Fearon, James, and David Laitin. "Neotrusteeship and the Problem of Weak States." *International Security* 28, no. 4 (Spring 2004): 5–43.

First Annual Report of the Boston Educational Commission for Freedmen. Boston: David Clapp, 1863.

First Annual Report of the National Freedman's Relief Association. New York, 1863.

Fleming, Walter. "Forty Acres and a Mule." *North American Review* 183 (May 1906): 721–737.

Foner, Eric. *Reconstruction: America's Unfinished Revolution, 1863–1877.* New York: Harper and Row, 1988.

Foote, Shelby. *The Civil War: A Narrative.* 3 vols. New York: Random House, 1958–1974.

French, Austa. *Slavery in South Carolina and the Ex-Slaves: Or The Port Royal Mission.* New York: Winchell French, 1862.

Fukuyama, Francis. *State-Building: Governance and World Order in the 21st Century*. Ithaca, NY: Cornell University Press, 2004.

Fukuyama, Francis. *Nation-Building: Beyond Afghanistan and Iraq*. Baltimore: The Johns Hopkins University Press, 2006.

Fukuyama, Francis. "Liberalism versus State-Building." *Journal of Democracy* 18, no. 3 (July 2007): 10–13.

Garry, Ann, and Marilyn Pearsall. *Women, Knowledge, and Reality: Explorations in Feminist Philosophy*. New York: Routledge, 1996.

Goldfield, David et al. *The American Journey*. Upper Saddle River, NJ: Prentice Hall, 2002.

Goldstein, Joshua, and Jon Pevehouse. *International Relations*. New York: Longman, 2010.

Greenhill, Kelly, and Solomon Major. "The Perils of Profiling: Civil War Spoilers and the Collapse of Intrastate Accords." *International Security* 31, no. 3 (Winter 2006–2007): 7–40.

Headley, Phineas Camp. *The Patriot Boy: or, The Life and Career of Major-General Ormsby M. Mitchel*. New York: W. H. Appleton, 1865.

Helsley, Alexia Jones. *Beaufort, South Carolina: A History*. Charleston, SC: The History Press, 2005.

Howard, Oliver. *Autobiography of Oliver Otis Howard*. New York: Baker and Taylor, 1875.

Huntington, Samuel. *Political Order in Changing Societies*. New Haven, CT: Yale University Press, 2006.

Jacoway, Elizabeth. *Yankee Missionaries in the South: The Penn School Experiment*. Baton Rouge: Louisiana State University Press, 1980.

Johnson, Chalmers. *Japan: Who Governs?: The Rise of the Developmental State*. New York: W. W. Norton, 1994.

Johnson, Guion Griffis. *A Social History of the Sea Islands*. Chapel Hill: University of North Carolina Press, 1930.

Joint Publication 1-02, *Department of Defense Dictionary of Military and Associated Terms*. Washington, DC: Joint Chiefs of Staff, 2010.

Joint Publication 3-0, *Operations*. Washington, DC: Joint Chiefs of Staff, 2006.

Joint Publication 3-07.6, *Joint Tactics, Techniques, and Procedures for Foreign Humanitarian Assistance*. Washington, DC: Joint Chiefs of Staff, 2001.

Joint Publication 5-0, *Joint Operational Planning*. Washington, DC: Joint Chiefs of Staff, 2006.

Jones, Virgil. *The Civil War at Sea*. 3 vols. New York: Holt, Rinehart, Winston, 1961.

Kanbur, Ravi. "What's Social Policy Got to Do with Economic Growth?" Draft paper available at http://www.arts.cornell.edu/poverty/kanbur/SocPolEconGrowth.pdf, 2006.

Kapoor, Ilan. "Participatory Development, Complicity, and Desire." *Third World Quarterly* 26, no. 8 (2005): 1203–1220.

Kibler, Lilian. *Benjamin F. Perry: South Carolina Unionist.* Durham, NC: Duke University Press, 1946.

Levine, Robert, ed. *Martin R. Delany: A Documentary Reader.* Chapel Hill: University of North Carolina Press, 2003.

Mansfield, Edward, and Jack Snyder. "The Sequencing 'Fallacy.'" *Journal of Democracy* 18, no. 3 (July 2007): 5–10.

Marshall, George. "Remarks by the Secretary of State." Harvard University, Cambridge, MA, June 5, 1947.

McFeely, William. *Yankee Stepfather: General O. O. Howard and the Freedmen.* New York: W. W. Norton, 1994.

Mearsheimer, John. "The Only Exit from Bosnia." *New York Times*, October 7, 1997, A31.

Miller, Edward. *Gullah Statesman: Robert Smalls from Slavery to Congress, 1839–1915.* Columbia: University of South Carolina Press, 1995.

Miller, Paul. "The Case for Nation-Building: Why and How to Fix Failed States." *Prism* 3, no. 1 (December 2011): 63–74.

Miller, Randall. "Introduction. The Freedmen's Bureau and Reconstruction: An Overview." In *The Freedmen's Bureau and Reconstruction: Reconsiderations*, ed. Paul Cimbala and Randall Miller, xiii–xxxii. New York: Fordham University Press, 1999.

Mjagkij, Nina. *Organizing Black America: An Encyclopedia of African American Associations.* New York: Routledge, 2001.

Natsios, Andrew. "The Nine Principles of Reconstruction and Development." *Parameters* 35, no. 3 (Autumn 2005): 4–20.

New England Freedmen's Aid Society. *Circular*, October 20, 1865, Boston, MA: New England Freedmen's Aid Society, 1865.

Ochiai, Akiko. "The Port Royal Experiment Revisited: Northern Visions of Reconstruction and the Land Question." *New England Quarterly* 74, no. 1 (March 2001): 94–117.

The Office of the United Nations High Commissioner for Refugees. *The State of the World's Refugees: Human Displacement in the New Millennium.* New York: Oxford University Press, 2006.

Paris, Roland. *At War's End: Building Peace after Civil Conflict.* New York: Cambridge University Press, 2004.

Pearson, Elizabeth. *Letters from Port Royal: Written at the Time of the Civil War.* Boston: W. B. Clarke, 1906.

Pease, William. "Three Years among the Freedmen: William C. Garnett and the Port Royal Experiment." *Journal of Negro History* 42 (1957): 98–117.

Pennsylvania Freedmen's Relief Association: FRA Report of the Proceedings of a Meeting Held at Concert Hall, Philadelphia: On Tuesday Evening, November 3, 1863, to Take into Consideration the Condition of the Freed People of the South. Philadelphia: Merrihew and Thompson, 1863.

Pickering, Jeffrey, and Mark Peceny. "Forging Democracy at Gunpoint." *International Studies Quarterly* 50 no. 3 (2006): 539–559.

Pierce, Edward. *The Negroes at Port Royal: Report of E. L. Pierce, Government Agent, to the Hon. Salmon P. Chase, Secretary of the Treasury.* Boston: R. F. Wallcut, 1862.

Pierce, Edward. "The Freedmen at Port Royal." *North American Review* 101 no. 208 (July 1865): 1–28.

Pollard, Edward. *The Lost Cause.* New York: E. B. Treat, 1867.

Poole, W. Scott. "Religion, Gender, and the Lost Cause in South Carolina's 1876 Governor's Race: 'Hampton or Hell!'" *Journal of Southern History* 68, no. 3 (August 2002): 573–578.

Pugh, Jonathan. "Social Transformation and Participatory Planning in St. Lucia." *Royal Geographical Society* 37, no. 4 (2005): 384–392.

Rachal, John. "Gideonites and Freedmen: Adult Literacy Education at Port Royal, 1862–1865." *Journal of Negro Education* 55, no. 4 (Autumn 1986): 453–469.

Reiter, Dan. "Does Peace Nurture Democracy?" *Journal of Politics* 63, no. 3 (August 2001): 935–948.

Richardson, E. Allen. "Architects of a Benevolent Empire: The Relationship between the American Missionary Association and the Freedmen's Bureau in Virginia, 1865–1872." In *The Freedmen's Bureau and Reconstruction: Reconsiderations,* ed. Paul Cimbala and Randall Miller, 119–139. New York: Fordham University Press, 1999.

Roark, James. *Masters without Slaves: Southern Planters in the Civil War and Reconstruction.* New York: W. W. Norton, 1977.

Roper, Laura Wood. "Frederick Law Olmsted and the Port Royal Experiment." *Journal of Southern History* 31, no. 3 (August 1965): 272–284.

Rose, Willie Lee. *Rehearsal for Reconstruction: The Port Royal Experiment.* New York: Bobbs-Merrill, 1965.

Rosengarten, Theodore. *Tombee: Portrait of a Cotton Planter.* New York: William Morrow, 1986.

Saville, Julie. *The Work of Reconstruction: From Slave to Wage Laborer in South Carolina, 1860–1870.* New York: Cambridge University Press, 1994.

Schmidt, James. "'A Full-Fledged Government of Men': Freedmen's Bureau Labor Policy in South Carolina, 1865–1868." In *The Freedmen's Bureau and Reconstruction: Reconsiderations,* ed. Paul Cimbala and Randall Miller, 219–260. New York: Fordham University Press, 1999.

Second Annual Report of the New England Freedmen's Aid Society (Educational Commission): Presented to the Society, April 21, 1864. Boston: Office of the Society, 1864.

Sellers, L. Earnest. "Robert Smalls: Civil War Hero." *Negro Digest* (April 1964): 24–28.

Shapiro, Herbert. "The Ku Klux Klan during Reconstruction: The South Carolina Episode." *Journal of Negro History* 49, no. 1 (January 1964): 34–55.

Sherman, William. *Memoirs.* New York: D. Appleton, 1875.

Shiva, Vandana. *Staying Alive: Women, Ecology, and Development.* London: Zed Books, 1988.

Simkins, Francis. "The Ku Klux Klan in South Carolina, 1868–1871." *Journal of Negro History* 12, no. 4 (October 1927): 606–647.

Simkins, Francis, and Robert Woody. *South Carolina during Reconstruction.* Chapel Hill: University of North Carolina Press, 1932.

Simmons, P. J. "Learning to Live with NGOs." *Foreign Policy* 112 (Fall 1998): 82–96.

Simonson, Lynnell, and Virginia Bushaw. "Participatory Action Research: Easier Said Than Done." *American Sociologist* 24, no. 1 (1993): 27–37.

Stedman, Stephen. "Spoiler Problems in Peace Processes." *International Security* 22, no. 2 (Fall 1997): 5–53.

Stein, Barry. "Durable Solutions for Developing Country Refugees." *International Migration Review* 20, no. 2 (Summer 1986): 264–282.

Stewart, Rory, and Gerald Knaus. *Can Intervention Work?* New York: W. W. Norton, 2011.

Stone, H. David. *Vital Rails: The Charleston & Savannah Railroad and the Civil War in South Carolina.* Columbia: University of South Carolina Press, 2008.

Sumner, Andy, and Michael Tribe. *International Development Studies: Theories and Methods in Research and Practice.* Los Angeles: Sage Publications, 2008.

Suri, Jeremi. *Liberty's Surest Guardian.* New York: Free Press, 2011.

Taylor, Kay Ann. "Mary S. Peake and Charlotte L. Forten: Black Teachers during the Civil War and Reconstruction." *Journal of Negro Education* 74, no. 2 (Spring 2005): 124–137.

Thomas, Emory. *The Confederate Nation.* New York: Harper and Row, 1979.

Thomas, Emory. *Robert E. Lee.* New York: W. W. Norton, 1995.

Towne, Laura. *Letters and Diary of Laura Towne,* ed. Rupert Sargent Holland. Cambridge, MA: Riverside Press, 1912.

Trinkley, Michael, and Debi Hacker. *The Archaeological Manifestations of the "Port Royal Experiment" at Mitchelville, Hilton Head, South Carolina.* Columbia, SC: Chicora Foundation, 1987.

Trowbridge, J. T. *The South: A Tour of Its Battlefields and Ruined Cities.* Hartford, CT: L. Stebbins, 1866.

Tucker, David. "Facing the Facts: The Failure of Nation Assistance." *Parameters* 23 (Summer 1993), 34–40.

U.S. Army Forces, Somalia, 10th Mountain Division (LI). *After Action Report, Summary.* Fort Drum, New York: Headquarters, 10th Mountain Division, 1993.

Uvin, Peter, Pankaj Jain, and L. David Brown. *Scaling Up NGO Programs in India: Strategies and Debates.* Boston: Institute for Development Research, 2000.

Van Doren Stern, Philip. *The Confederate Navy: A Pictorial History.* Garden City, NY: Doubleday, 1962.

The War of the Rebellion: A Compilation of the Official Records of the Union and Confederate Armies. Washington, DC: Government Printing Office, 1880–1901.

Warner, Ezra. *Generals in Blue: Lives of the Union Commanders.* Baton Rouge: Louisiana State University Press, 1964.

Waters, Tony. *The Persistence of Subsistence Agriculture: Life Beneath the Level of the Marketplace.* Lanham, MD: Lexington Books, 2006.

Weddle, Kevin. *Lincoln's Tragic Admiral: The Life of Samuel Francis Du Pont.* Charlottesville: University of Virginia Press, 2005.

Weigley, Russell. *The American Way of War.* Bloomington: University of Indiana Press, 1973.

Wesley, John. *Thoughts upon Slavery.* London: R. Hawes, 1774.

Wesley, John. *The Works of the Reverend John Wesley, A. M.* New York: J. Emory and B. Waugh, 1831.

Williams, Alfred. "General Wade Hampton Campaigns in the 'Black Belt.'" In *Port Royal under Six Flags*, ed. Katharine Jones, 312–316. Indianapolis: Bobbs-Merrill, 1960.

Wolf, Kurt. "Laura M. Towne and the Freed People of South Carolina, 1862–1901." *South Carolina Historical Magazine* 98, no. 4 (October 1997): 375–405.

Wright, Donald, and Timothy Reese. *On Point II: Transition to the New Campaign: The United States Army in Operation Iraqi Freedom, May 2003–January 2005.* Fort Leavenworth, KS: Combat Studies Institute Press, 2008.

Zeitlin, Marian et al. *Strengthening the Family—Implications for International Development.* New York: United Nations University Press, 1995.

Zuczek, Richard. *State of Rebellion: Reconstruction in South Carolina.* Columbia: University of South Carolina Press, 1996.

Index

CPSIA information can be obtained
at www.ICGtesting.com
Printed in the USA
FSHW021724050920
73599FS